TROUBLESOME
BIBLE
PASSAGES

Volume 2

Randy Cross

Troublesome Bible Passages
Volume 2

Lessons From 23 Familiar Texts

Copyright © 1997 by Abingdon Press

ISBN 0-687-06173-3

This book is printed on acid-free paper.

Manufactured in the United States of America.

Cover photograph: FPG International

98 99 00 01 02 03 04 05 06— 2 3 4 5 6 7 8 9 10

Abingdon Press
Nashville

Contents

From the Editor

Welcome to TROUBLESOME BIBLE PASSAGES, VOLUME 2. We have included in this volume eight Scriptures from the Old Testament and fifteen from the New Testament and encourage you to take a fresh, new look at passages that may be familiar and unfamiliar to you at the same time.

How can the Holy Scriptures, which are a gift from God for our growth in grace and faith, be considered "troublesome"? These twenty-three passages may be called troublesome for one of several reasons. The Scripture

- appears to contradict other Scripture;
- is problematic in its theological implications;
- uses difficult language or uncommon imagery;
- appears so lodged in its original cultural setting that it seems confusing or out of date for modern readers.

You may have heard these Scripture references many times; now they can come alive for you with insights and understanding that you never had before. Each passage is explained in its own context in the section "Words for Bible Times" (with added information in the leader's guide). More contemporary approaches are considered in the section "Words for Our Times," and the personal touch for you is added in the section "Words for My Life." The teaching plan in the leader's guide provides ways to study the Scripture from each of these three approaches and includes numerous discussion questions to focus and sustain an investigation into these passages.

We pray that your study of these Scriptures enriches your understanding and faith and leads you into a deeper relationship with Jesus Christ.

1

What Is the "Image of God" in Which We Are Created?

Genesis 1:26-31

Then God said, "Let us make humankind in our image, according to our likeness."

Genesis 1:26

WORDS FOR BIBLE TIMES

In the first five-and-a-half days of Creation, God said, "Let there be . . ." and there was light, sky, land, plants, stars, the sun and the moon, birds, fish, and animals. All of these were unbelievably magnificent creations, brought into being simply by God's Word.

On the last half of the sixth day, the work of Creation pauses for a moment, as God thinks about what this next and last creation will be. "Let us make humankind in our image."

The "us" in "Let us make" could either be a result of God's chatting with the angels that surround God or possibly a way that God uses the first person plural to refer to self before Creation—when *Us* was all there was. It could even be a phrase whose understanding has been lost over the centuries since the time these words were first written.

The important thing about the verse is—God thinks for a moment before creating in God's own image! Imagine any potentially life-changing decision you have had to make. It is always good to take a moment to decide if it really is a good idea.

The word *image* is from the Latin word *imago*, which means "likeness, or semblance." As we look at this verse of Scripture, it is important to realize that God said, "image," not, "Let us make little gods that are just like me." *Image* may mean a likeness, but it certainly does not mean God created us to be essentially the same beings as God is. We are the creations, and God is the Creator.

However, God will give this human a special place, with dominion over the rest of creation. Created in God's image (male and female!), humankind also receives the first blessing from God to grow and receive all that God has given. "Be fruitful and multiply" are God's words, and they remind us of the precious gift we are given to be able to create families and communities and a world full of people. It is apparently a gift that we must care for in our lives.

As the work of Creation comes to a close, God takes a moment after all is said and done ("Let there be" and it was!) to look at everything that had been made, and we read the wonderful observation: "it was very good." From beginning to end, God has made a good world, with good humans.

WORDS FOR OUR TIME

We have a natural desire to want to know what someone looks like, imagining their physical characteristics, and that natural desire extends to our looking for God. When I was four years old, I thought God must look like the actor who played the private investigator, Paul Drake, on the television show "Perry Mason." Somebody, somewhere had told me God had grey hair, and Paul Drake was the only grey-haired person I had seen who I thought "ought" to look like God. That was four-year-old thinking, however. Adults should do better.

As the second of the Ten Commandments, God warned the children of Israel not to make "any graven image" (King James Version), no carved idols of wood or stone that could be displayed as God. The God who brought the Israelites to freedom from slavery had no clear physical form that could be captured or limited in an image. The prophets also warned Israel against bowing down and worshiping images and idols, in the way that the Canaanites and others worshiped the idols of Baal, Ashteroth, and others as their gods. As we think about being "created in God's image," we can assume that God does not like the idea of our claiming a physical image of what God looks like.

Even more, if we were to think about the "image of God" as physical, we would have trouble deciding which "physical image" it would be. To tell the truth, you and I simply do not look alike. From hair color to eyes, from gender, skin, height, weight, to all of our physical characteristics, there are subtle and significant differences among human beings. Even identical twins are not absolutely identical. Somewhere there is a mole or freckle out of place.

Apparently, then, when God said "in our image," God did not mean physical characteristics. Over the centuries people have wanted to picture God using all kinds of physical characteristics. Usually, they tried to make God look like their particular group or sex or skin color. What they were doing, however, was actually trying to "make God in our image."

God is by nature a spiritual Being who creates with a voice and whose power and likeness is beyond physical limitations. Since we are created in the image of the God who is Spirit, we imitate God and reflect that createdness as we live out our spiritual life and power. It makes much more sense to think about how we are like each other spiritually and how we are like God in a spiritual way. God loves, and we love. God creates, redeems, and sustains—so do we. We describe God with other words such as *faith, reason, justice, forgiveness, the capacity to dream,* and *joy.* We believe these and others are part of God's essential nature. We "look like God" and live up to our created image as these characteristics describe us in our lives.

On the other hand, when we are selfish, self-centered, unjust, unforgiving, and act as though nothing in life really matters, is creative, or redeeming, then we blur or shadow God's image in us. We stop living the way we have been created. When we act this way, and others look at us, and as we look in our own mirrors, it gets hard to see our lives as resembling God. You have to wonder if perhaps as God paused before creating us, God pondered *Can these humans truly live up to their part in creation? Can my image be seen in them?* Even if God thought so, God trusted us enough to go ahead and bless us. It is up to us to live that title.

WORDS FOR MY LIFE

We have a life-task that is tied to our createdness in the image of God. We have been given the ability and the charge of caring for the earth. The word in Genesis is *dominion*, which means "rule and authority," the way a queen or a king would rule. Realize, however, that although a queen rules a country, she does not really own it in the end. She will die someday, and someone else will rule. As the old saying goes, "You can't take it with you." Ownership is always temporary. Dominion, then, does not mean ownership, but stewardship. Created in God's image, we are given the responsibility to use everything in our power to be stewards or caretakers, careful managers of the creation entrusted to us by God. All humans have been blessed with the work of caring for the fish to birds to every living animal and plant in our world. We live out the image of God as we carefully and deliberately love this creation of God.

We are not just given a job, however, as if God needed custodians to keep the earth picked up and dusted. You and I are also supposed to enjoy this world, to use it, and to be part of it. As we camp, or ski, or see the beauty created for our eyes, it should bring us joy. As we grow crops (watch out for the apple trees!), live in our homes, and watch with amazement as new creatures are found in the depths of the ocean, we are brought to a sense of praise to God for the great things God has done. In Psalm 8, the writer proclaims how excellent God's creation is, how human beings are woven into the world in a special way, and that God is mindful of us. Joy and care are linked in the role of stewards in the image of God.

Does that happen, however? Sometimes it seems the world is treated more like something that is owned by its inhabitants, instead of cherished by its stewards. We are acquainted with the words *recycling, ecology,* and others; but so much of our world is not cared for in a very loving way. We have an opportunity in our world today to destroy it through our powerful technology and lack of care. As humans continue to "be fruitful and multiply," the pressure on the resources of the earth that have existed for eons will continue to mount.

How do I personally live as a steward of all God has created? How do my family's decisions reflect our understanding of living in God's image in this created world? When my neighbors and my community make choices about landfills, developments, and the use of the world's resources, are those choices in line with our charge to have dominion and not ownership over the earth? The fact is, when just you and I decide that we will treat our world poorly, we have failed our task as caretakers of creation, and we have failed to live up to our created image.

Strangely enough, with our modern, technological world, we have the opportunity as perhaps never before to truly manage our world's resources and treasures. We are able creatively to grow and produce what is needed for our lives and to do so in ways that do not destroy or injure the creation given to our care. The challenge is, we must have the heart as individuals, communities, societies, and the world to enjoy our earth, but to cherish it as well. We must have the heart of a steward, in the image of God.

2

Why Did God Choose Abel and Not Cain?

Genesis 4:1-16

And the LORD had regard for Abel and his offering, but for Cain and his offering he had no regard.

Genesis 4:4-5

WORDS FOR BIBLE TIMES

The story of Cain and Abel tells of the world's first death, not by accident, but by murder. It is the story of jealousy, and anger, and sin. The entire attention of the story focuses on Cain, the older of Adam and Eve's sons. Cain is a farmer, and Abel is a shepherd.

Sadly enough, the recording of the first murder begins with a time of worship. The two brothers decide that they need to worship God and make an offering. For some reason, Cain's offering is turned down. This seems to put in motion all the events that follow, which result in Abel's blood being spilled on the ground in the field.

The question for this troublesome Bible passage is, Why did God choose Abel and not Cain? Some who have studied these verses have believed Cain's rejection came because he only brought "an offering," whereas Abel brought the very best of the firstlings of his flock. Since this is the world's first offering, though, without any previous rules for how offerings are to be made, it seems a bit unfair to old Cain to have his offering rejected simply because he did not know any better.

Other scholars believe that the rejection of Cain rested in the heart and manner of his giving over against Abel's. Abel thought enough to carefully bring the best he had, which showed a deeper reverence to God. Cain just made an offering.

Are we so sure that God chose Abel and not Cain? When it appears that the offering is rejected, God goes to Cain to counsel, to encourage, and even to warn him that sin is "lurking" and waiting for a chance to master Cain. God does not say a word to Abel.

The core of this story seems to go beyond God's rejection or acceptance of the two brothers to the warning that God brings to Cain concerning the potential for sin in his life. God's hope for the children of Adam and Eve is that they would avoid the trap into which their parents fell. The seed of revenge and violence was already planted in Cain and was starting to grow.

We might say that it was Cain who rejected God. Cain made the choice to listen to his own heart, which told him to hate, to envy, and to kill his brother. Instead of guarding against sin, Cain welcomed the sin.

"Sin" can be defined as "separation from God." The "sins" that we perform in our lives are only signs and results of the more fundamental breaking away of our hearts from God's. Cain broke away. The natural action to follow was that he would kill his brother.

Even then, God did not reject Cain! Even as God heard the blood of Abel crying out from the same ground that had produced the first offering that Cain brought in worship, God still does not abandon Cain. Granted, Cain will have to face the consequences for such horrible, sin-full actions. Cain is banished from that ground. God, however, answers Cain's fear that anyone can kill him (for he belongs nowhere) by placing God's mark, God's claim on Cain, and proclaiming that here the killing must end. Is that a rejection? Or is it better seen as God's caring for Cain in a powerful way, even as Cain gave himself to sin?

WORDS FOR OUR TIME

Poor Cain! He just was not treated properly! He did what he thought was right, but God chose his brother's offering instead! You cannot really blame Cain for being angry, maybe not even for having that anger consume him and lead him to want to get back at his brother. Sure, he probably should not have been violent, and murder is a horrible thing; but look at Cain's life. Poor Cain.

Do we look for excuses to sin? Are we prone to set ourselves apart from God's creative and sustaining love? It surely appears so. When we see something that we desire, how often do we act with only our own interests in mind—sort of a "me first" attitude? Our "countenance" falls when things do not go our way, and we start looking for someone to blame besides ourselves, someone to receive our anger and wrath.

"Original sin" refers to our tendency as humans to act and live separated from the love and will of God. We must "guard" against that tendency, or we will certainly do what Adam, Eve, Cain, and every other human has done. We will sin.

The issue of this Bible story is not so much that God accepted or rejected an offering, but rather what Cain—and we—must do when faced with something in life that goes contrary to what we had planned or hoped or intended. The fact is, the bringing of the offering in the story represents many things in your life and mine that we perhaps fail at.

Is sin to be a natural consequence of our failures? Does violence against another person naturally follow a disappointment? Our challenge is to decide what we will do and how we will act when faced with a life that is not guaranteed to go our way all the time. What will be our response when things we do are rejected? "Sin crouches at the door" of our lives just as surely as at Cain's.

Cain made a sad mistake that was the core to his sinful act against his brother. Cain somehow decided that God's acceptance or rejection of his offering meant God's acceptance or rejection of Cain. That was wrong. Cain also decided that the rejection of his offering was worth more than his own brother's life. That was wrong, as well. Apparently God loved Cain and loves us even when the things we do fall short of what God intends for us. God also expects that we will love each other much more than the successes or failures or conflicts that occur between us.

WORDS FOR MY LIFE

I have always thought that bullies show a consistent lack of imagination and a lack of real control in dealing with the world that does not always go their way. I have been on the receiving end of "fallen countenances" in junior high school, when on occasion, a typically huge "Cain-like" person decided that someone close by needed to pay for his own shortcomings. I have come to realize since that time that a boy or a girl normally is taught about the use of violence—whether it is appropriate or not appropriate. The teaching usually occurs by the actions or lack of action by a parent or significant adult in the child's life. What have you taught your children or grandchildren about the use of violence?

One of the rules of the Cross home is that absolutely, totally, completely—violence is not an option. You can be angry, or frustrated, or even furious; but you are not allowed to be violent in our home. Besides the obvious reasons of people getting hurt when violence is allowed, we have that rule to allow our sons—and Mom and Dad—to find another way to deal with disappointments and the basic challenges of living together in one place. When violence is the first option, nothing creative or loving can have room to grow. We try to "guard against sin" at least in this one way. It is interesting how, even with that rule, now and then an argument at home boils into a fight, usually between two sons. It requires some quick intervention and a cooling-down time to help them remember who they are.

Who are they? They are the sons of Randy and Cheri Cross and children of God. Both of those family groups cherish life and peace and the individual apart from what he or she has done. Perhaps the greatest gift we can give to future generations is to help create homes and relationships in which the person is valued and violence is eliminated.

3

What Is the Sabbath Day, and How Should I Observe It?

Deuteronomy 5:12-15

The seventh day is a sabbath to the LORD your God; you shall not do any work.

Deuteronomy 5:14

WORDS FOR BIBLE TIMES

The word *sabbath* in Hebrew means "to strike," as in a labor strike against a factory. It means "to not work" as an intentional decision and not because there is simply nothing to do. *Shabbat Shalom* is the greeting one Jew gives to another during that seventh day of the week; and it means, of course, the peace of the sabbath—or better, the "peace of the time of rest."

Our Scripture for this lesson is part of Deuteronomy's version of the Ten Commandments. (They are also located in Exodus 20.) The Ten Commandments are rules of life that are given to us and to the nation of Israel for our own good. Some of the commandments deal with our relationship with God, and some deal with our place in the community. The commandment of keeping the sabbath involves both God and the community. As such, it becomes a focal point in the Ten Commandments between our two critical relationships in life: our relationship with God and the way in which our lives blend with others.

The Israelites had just spent 430 years in slavery in Egypt (Exodus 12:40). Seven days a week, sunup to sundown, they had worked as human machines to build the cities of the pharaohs. There was time only to sleep and to recover a few moments of life. There was no time to worship God, nor to cherish the life of family and community as a source of joy and peace.

The word of freedom came to the Israelites, and they crossed the Red Sea. As they settled at Mount Sinai, God gave to them through Moses a set of commandments that not only would guide them in living a more holy and peaceful life but that would give them a unique identity as God's chosen people. The sabbath was unique to Israel, with a seven-day cycle of living that included one-seventh of the time given over to resting. Did you read why the sabbath was given? "Remember that you were a slave in the land of Egypt, and the LORD your God brought you out from there with a mighty hand and an outstretched arm" (Deuteronomy 5:15). The Israelites are to keep the sabbath as a constant weekly reminder of the time in which they had no rest, but were slaves. As they keep the sabbath, they are able to see the rest of the week as holy and a gift from God as they live now in freedom.

The Deuteronomy passage is very specific about the keeping of the sabbath. In fact, it is the longest of all the Ten Commandments in its explanation, which may give us another insight as to its importance. Sons, daughters, slaves, oxen, donkeys, livestock, and even the resident aliens in the town are to "strike from work"—everyone is to rest. The sabbath commandment is perhaps the best commandment to show how the Israelites were to keep their faith corporately. It is not enough for me, or just for you, to rest that day. Together, as a whole community, we are faithful as the seventh day is kept from work. Together we are a unique people, the Israelites say.

The only two hints that we are given in the Scripture that this sabbath day is to be different are these:

- you shall not do any work
- you are to keep it holy

The commandment is very specific about not working and about who shall refrain from the labor that typifies the rest of the week. However, it does not clearly define what is meant by "keeping it holy." God does not command, "You shall go to church both morning and evening and not play cards or dance on that day." We need to know that God also does not say, "Keep a couple of hours in the morning as church time, and then go and do what you want."

"Observe the sabbath day and keep it holy." The day for the Israelites was holy, in part, because no work happened. With time on their hands that day, they were able to reclaim their family and to dwell for a time on the Source of all holiness, as they worshiped God and spent time in study and contemplation. The greatest gift of the day of the sabbath was that the Israelites had time to do all of that, because they were no longer slaves.

WORDS FOR OUR TIME

How busy are you?

If your schedule is like mine, you are already planning activities months ahead and wishing that you could have gotten to other jobs or tasks months before. There is always something to do!

On top of that, someone went out and discovered electricity. With the invention of the light bulb, we can now work without stopping, if only we could physically do so. Days off and weekends become "to-do" lists, or a time of running to different sports and recreational activities, with just enough time to turn around and drive to work on Monday morning (well rested?).

God has a different idea in mind. God knows that we can lose our lives in a world so well scheduled. We are almost like the Israelites in Egypt, except that perhaps we are not building cities for the pharaohs.

God's commandment to the people of faith (a commandment, remember, and not merely a suggestion) is to rest. Once a week, take the time to recover your life. Take a day in seven to renew your bond with God, with your family, and with your world.

However, the word *sabbath* does not mean "a day off," as if the core of your life is your work, and that once a week, you get to take a break from it. As people of faith, our life's center ought to be the living God. The sabbath becomes a time set aside from all the business in order to rest and be renewed in the uncluttered presence of God. "Observe the sabbath day and keep it holy" means that we take special care on that one day to be aware of God's holiness in our lives. It means we move into a holy time, of "being still and knowing" who God is.

Almost everything in our world, however, ignores that need and call to a holy time. I do not believe it is an intentional destroying of the sabbath as much as it is a thoughtless filling up of every part of our society's life with things to do. It is easy to wake up on a sabbath morning and plan to be as busy as any other day.

The ease with which that happens makes it seductive. We begin to fill up the open space created by the sabbath that was meant for rest and renewal in the presence of God. We fill it up with everything else. We do not call it enslavement, but that is exactly what happens. If we intend to hear the word of God and to discern the will of God for our lives, we desperately need to observe the sabbath, to keep it uncluttered and holy.

WORDS FOR MY LIFE

There is an important reason for nap time in preschool, you know. I suppose partly it is to give the teacher a bit of a break. More importantly, though, rest time allows busy preschool minds and bodies to rest for a bit before they become busy again.

In times of crisis or danger, we might find it necessary to go without rest for a while. But you and I have been created in such a way that we must rest, or we will simply die.

Most of the things I do in my life are important, by the way. Some of them really are things that folks are counting on me to do! However, I have enough business right now to keep me in a state of business for a number of years, it seems. If I wanted it to be so, I could move my life into permanent "crisis mode," never getting any rest, and still not get everything done.

So when do we rest? A better question may be, to whom do we become slaves and to whom do we offer our first loyalties in our lives? The two most important things about sabbath are that

- it is a time for us to stop doing our business and recover our sense of balance and peace in the world;
- it reminds us that we belong to God; we are not slaves to anyone or anything else.

When we observe the sabbath and keep it holy, we keep ourselves connected to God's healing and strengthening love.

I said that there are two important things. There is really a third important thing, however. If I honestly and intentionally keep the sabbath and allow it to have a powerful, central role in my life, it should naturally follow that I will invite others to take time to rest in their lives as well. As I take time in "holy idleness," the persons I am normally "busy with" can rest, too. If a meeting I need to have is not scheduled for a sabbath, then everyone else is freed. The opposite is also true. As others take time to rest and be re-created by God, I do not feel the pressure to have to work during that same time.

God gave the sabbath commandment to the people of Israel, and not just to individuals, because a corporate rest does the world a world of good.

4

Does God Cause the Events of History?

Ezra 1:1-4

In the first year of King Cyrus of Persia, in order that the word of the LORD by the mouth of Jeremiah might be accomplished, the LORD stirred up the spirit of King Cyrus.

Ezra 1:1

WORDS FOR BIBLE TIMES

Nebuchadnezzar was the ruler of the Babylonian Empire. Instead of turning the conquered kingdom of Judah into a vassal state, he decided to take the majority of the population of Israel back to Babylonia. The people had been without a home and without the Temple for seventy years now.

Nebuchadnezzar's kingdom came to an end, however, as Cyrus, king of the Persian Empire, extended his rule over Babylonia. In the first year of his reign in Babylonia, Cyrus became almost a "transplanted Moses" as he proclaimed, "Let the people of the God of Israel go!" Actually, his words are translated a bit differently: "The LORD, the God of heaven" has given him a task, a charge: to build God a house in Jerusalem, in Judah. He freed all who would worship God to go back to Jerusalem and rebuild the Temple that was destroyed seventy years before. The surviving children of Israel were to be assisted with gold, silver, goods, animals, and offerings to help build the house.

What a strange thing to happen! Cyrus was not a Jew. Judah was not a fine piece of captured real estate to worry about reestablishing a large population there. Why go to all the trouble of freeing captives, sending them back to their homeland, and then giving them authority and resources to build a new worship center for their faith?

The answer is, there is no good reason to do such a thing—except for the fact that God somehow moved in Cyrus's life to create that proclamation.

The question for our lesson is, Does God cause the events of history? It is a complex topic. On one hand, if we answer no, then to be consistent we have to view God as simply a watcher of the world's events, what some have called a cosmic clockmaker. This clockmaker has set the world spinning and now sits back and watches it tick. As we see God in the Scripture, in the tradition of our faith and in our own experiences, that image of God is hard to justify.

Even in our prayers, we ask God to intercede and to change the world at least in small ways. To believe that God is a once-upon-a-time creator, redeemer, and sustainer, but who now is only a watching God, does not fill us with hope that the future is in God's hands.

On the other hand, if we answer that yes, God does cause the events of history, then immediately we have to ask why earthquakes, war, famine, floods, tornadoes, and accidents occur in our world. If God truly does have the power and the inclination to cause events in history, why would God choose somehow to not act or to act against the work and the hope of goodness in this world?

We still have Cyrus, however, sounding as though God is creating the change in history. The fact is, the Babylonian Exile ended. The Jews were allowed to return to their home and to rebuild the Temple. Throughout the Scripture, we find all sorts of examples pointing to God's intervention. We find examples of God's initiation of blessing and salvation in the course of history. We believe that even Jesus' life is a historical event, caused by God.

The key to today's Scripture comes in the way the writer describes the motivation for Cyrus's action: "The LORD stirred up the spirit of King Cyrus of Persia." God's action to free the Jews from captivity in Babylonia came as God "stirred" Cyrus's heart, motivating Cyrus to act as a redeemer for Israel. As Cyrus responded, freedom came. Nothing in the Scripture, however, makes it appear that Cyrus acted as a robot, without choice in his life. Cyrus cooperated with God, at God's initiative, but with Cyrus's permission and involvement.

WORDS FOR OUR TIME

As we look at the history of the Christian faith, we see so many events that have occurred in which God's hand appeared to be acting to bring about something good. When Paul met Jesus on the road to Damascus—as Paul was going to arrest Christians—he became the greatest missionary the early faith ever knew. Martin Luther wrestled within his life as a priest to find meaning for some of the church's practices. He was led to post his list of concerns on the church door, hoping for dialogue. Little did he know the impact that action would have on the church. After John Wesley failed miserably in his missionary trip to Georgia and struggled with his faith and God's grace, he went to Aldersgate and there had his heart "strangely warmed" with the assurance of God's grace and acceptance of him. That assurance helped Wesley move in faith to preach to the mining communities of England. Over and over again, we can look back in history and point to those events and say, "There was God."

Did you notice, however, in the three above examples, as with Cyrus, that God's involvement came in the changing of one life, one heart at a time? That one change then in turn changed countless others. Sometimes we would love to see God bringing a cosmic-changing miracle, like a thunderbolt or a whirling storm that would alter things in the world, and therefore prove God's existence, making the world more loving, just, and full of grace as a result.

That, however, is not God's way. Usually, God nudges, guides, and stirs our friends, neighbors, leaders, and even strangers to create a change in their own world. This changing of lives does shake the world from time to time. Faithful respondents to God's nudging bring about love, justice, and grace, using all that God has given them.

God's nudgings are not always very clear, however. Sometimes it takes quite a while before we can look back and see the evidence of God's work. Only later can we say with confidence that what has been accomplished, or where we have headed as a people or a church, has indeed been a result of God's intervention in our lives.

Where is God acting? That is a question of discernment. Someone being "nudged" by God needs to realize that he or she has not simply come up with a good idea, but that it is

God's idea and that God has issued an invitation to follow.

As people of faith in this world, we ought to pray constantly for God to "stir." As we look to the needs of the world, trouble spots, and things that we believe run counter to God's kingdom of love, grace, and justice, we are called to offer those things to God, with a prayer that God might move in the hearts of those who are in a position to make a difference. Granted, God may act anyway to create that change, but I believe God appreciates and cherishes the times when the children of God clearly and boldly shine a light on places and situations that need to be transformed by God's love.

WORDS FOR MY LIFE

Does God cause a change in the events of your life? I believe the answer is "Certainly!" Just as God acts on a world scale, so God can bring about a change for the better, a change for the best in your own life. God does so using the same tools of stirring and nudging.

When I finished college, I decided to move from North Dakota to Texas to begin seminary. I really had not made plans ever to go back to North Dakota. I needed a summer job, though. The day after I arrived in Texas, I received a phone call from a pastor in North Dakota, offering me a job as a summer youth pastor. The position would pay what I needed to have for school in the fall, and they would also take care of transportation and housing. I had never been to that particular church before, and I had only briefly met the pastor who called me and offered the job. I was nudged, however. It seemed to be the right thing to do, even though it would mean not spending the summer with my family as we had planned. I said yes to the offer and flew back to North Dakota for the summer. As a result of that moment, I made my home in North Dakota and have served six different congregations there. Most importantly, the day I arrived at the church, I met a young woman who four years later took me as her husband.

Did God cause all that to happen? Absolutely. Yet every step along the way, I had the opportunity to say no—that is, to not answer the stirring that was happening in my life.

When I begin to think of the thousands of people whose

lives have been affected in a ripple effect because of that one decision, it is staggering to imagine. Even more significant to me personally is when I think of how my life was drastically changed because of one yes.

You may be able to think of moments of decision that changed your life for the good for so many persons you know. Is there any reason to think that it was all just a coincidence, or a lucky choice? As a person of faith, and a follower of Christ, what a great opportunity you have to give thanks to God for the decision that God helped you to make!

It is critically important, however, that you and I take time to make ourselves ready to receive that "stirring" that God brings. A receptive spirit is loved by God, because God can begin the work of changing a life and even changing the world right away without having to persuade or convince that it is a good thing to do. God can work in anyone's life to bring about the change, but how much nicer it is when we offer ourselves as servants willing to be nudged and used.

As you think today about God's will for your life, is God stirring you? Taking the time to discern in your life God's work and will for you, and then having the courage and enthusiasm to say yes and begin the work, is one of the finest things you can ever do.

5

How Does God's Time Relate to Our Time?

Psalm 90

For a thousand years in your sight
　　are like yesterday when it is past,
or like a watch in the night.

Psalm 90:4

WORDS FOR BIBLE TIMES

No one can accuse the writer of Psalm 90 of having a big ego!

This psalm draws such a drastic difference between the majesty and eternity of God contrasted with the relative puny nature of humans, that we are left with almost a sense of irrelevance in the world and universe. Perhaps that is the purpose for this psalm.

Psalm 90 is the first psalm of the middle section of our Bible's collection of psalms. This section of psalms talks about the greatness of God; the need for the whole world (not just Israel) to praise God; how God's love and goodness are great; and finally, Israel's sin and the need to be forgiven by such a great God. If you were to read Psalms 90 through 106 in one sitting, you would find this collection to be a magnificent worship experience in writing and a masterful offering.

We are given Psalm 90 to figure out, however. As a way of beginning this section of the Book of Psalms, the ninetieth psalm offers a picture of God that is universe-sized. The psalmist is not satisfied to talk about a shepherd, or still waters, or even valleys—we are given the earth being formed, the mountains being brought forth, and a thousand years that seem to be just a brief moment for God.

The writer addresses God, but we get to eavesdrop and to decide whether we will agree with the writer's judgment. "You turn us back to dust," "you sweep them away; they are like a dream, / like grass that . . . fades and withers." Our normal human lifespan, the writer says to God, is seventy or eighty years; and it is soon gone. Apparently, the human being's life, of which normally we are so proud, with our accomplishments and greatness, is not nearly as great as we think it is, especially when set up against God's timeline.

Let us focus on God for a moment. God has been our dwelling place in all of the generations, and from everlasting to everlasting God is our God. Very simply, God is beyond our measurement, both in time and beyond time. There is something foreign about this description of God, as though God really is not like you and me.

That's the point. This psalm, which recognizes our humanness, places us in the clearly described place as "creature" or "creation." God is exactly who God is: the Creator of all and the Supreme Being in the universe. As such, God deals with time in a different way. Not limited by sunrises and sunsets, God exists in eternity, working in history only because that is all we humans can fully grasp. That a thousand years is viewed by God like a single portion of the night shows how much greater God is than we are.

It honestly puts us in our place, doesn't it? It certainly did so for the psalm writer. God's time, like God, is beyond our understanding. We use the word *eternity* with ease; but when we stop to think of an unending forever, with no beginning, even the word *eternity* pales as a full description.

The psalmist, when faced with the vast chasm between our way of existence and God's can only respond, "So teach us to count our days / that we may gain a wise heart" (verse 12). Instead of our time being spent counting our accomplishments and our grand plans for the world, it is better that we count our days and realize that, even with all the good that we do, wisdom comes in the understanding of our place (and our size) before God from whom all blessings flow.

WORDS FOR OUR TIME

In 1996, scientists were studying quasars using the Hubble Space Telescope. (A quasar is a starlike object.) The closest quasar was estimated to be tens of thousands of light years away. Like all things beyond our solar system, the distance has to be measured in time rather than in linear measurement. A light year is the distance light travels in a year. Instead of the quasars themselves being studied, scientists were really studying the remnants of light from thousands of years ago that only just now reached Earth. They were looking at the distant past.

What is eternity? It is the measurement of God's being. In comparison, we humans are like grass that grows in the morning and dies in the evening. Our "being" is a relatively minor length of time.

Wait a minute! Aren't you and I worth more than that? Look at all we as humans have accomplished over the past five or six thousand years! Look at our great inventions and thoughts. Yes, we have even been able to send human beings to the closest heavenly body to us—the moon—hundreds of thousands of miles away. But God's universe (to the extent we are aware of it!) expands to billions and billions of miles beyond miles. From everlasting to everlasting, God has been, and will be.

We have been very careful in our modern society to protect each other's egos and self-images. Among humans, that perhaps is an appropriate way to live. There is a tendency, however, to see ourselves and human beings in general as something far greater than we are. The folks building the tower of Babel had the same problem. Perhaps it is part of our human nature.

However, as we look at the entire universe, and as we begin to think about the quality and quantity of existence so far beyond our ability to measure or control that is found in the eternal with God, it may be that we have to set egos aside, and instead pick up a sense of awe, wonder, praise, and a realistic understanding of our fundamental need of God for our lives.

When we begin to see ourselves as the creatures of God (and not as gods ourselves!), we can begin to pray to God to "satisfy us in the morning with your steadfast love" and in the words of other verses from the psalm. Instead of having to control our world and time, we can begin to live graciously in the time that God gives us. We can take time to contemplate the incredible gift that is yet to come, which is—if you can believe it—eternal life in Christ.

WORDS FOR MY LIFE

"Just a second!" is a phrase heard around our house on a regular basis. Another phrase is "Hurry up—you'll be late!" Minutes become valuable in the moments before school starts. If you were to look at our family most days, you would call us "on the run." Our family is by no means the busiest in our city or our country. Many folks seem to be in a constant state of racing from one activity to another, putting off some important things because there is no time.

Our measurement of time in the modern world seems to be moving to increasingly smaller units. We now have split seconds, nanoseconds, and who knows what is next. It is worth mentioning, therefore, that if you "had time" to scan the Old Testament, you would find the word *hour* only four times in the King James Version (in the Book of Daniel) and not at all in the New Revised Standard Version. *Hour* is found in the New Testament (over seventy times), but never in the Bible do we find the words *minute* and *second* in terms of time measurement. *Day* is the standard division of time.

Today, however, every second counts. Minutes are valuable commodities. We constantly reset our clocks. We incessantly wonder what time it is. We tend to control our lives with such small parcels of time. "I can give you five minutes," as though it is something I own. Think about what happens to your congregation when the worship service runs "late" by a few minutes. Folks often use the phrase, "We are slaves to the clock," and "Time is money." We split our lives into such small segments that it may be possible that we are wasting our lives by shattering them, or at least turning them into just usable and expendable moments of existence.

However, this is the "day" that the Lord has made. It's amazing, isn't it, that with the unbelievable vastness of God's eternity, God has given you a day of life. God reaches us and calls us, not to use up our life-time, but to rejoice and be glad in it, to cherish it as a gift from the One who has made it. Instead of a twenty-four-hour measurement, *day* was a marking of life with the movement of the sun.

Can you recall a day in your past in which you let time go? It may have been a vacation or another special day in which you did not even look at your watch, but lived the entire day. I expect it was a holy time for you, and I also imagine you had more time than you realized. That is what happens when we reclaim "the day" from God, and use it, instead of using it up. We end up with less impatience, we are able to rest, and we are able to be more gracious in receiving and sharing the gifts that the day itself brings.

We live in such a busy world that it is critically important for you and me to see our time in the measurement of eternity. Up against that, what is important? Simply to let God's work be manifest in us and to gain a wise heart.

6

Are Our Lives Predetermined?

Psalm 139:13-18

In your book were written
all the days that were formed for me,
when none of them as yet existed.
Psalm 139:16b

WORDS FOR BIBLE TIMES

Psalm 139, when read with a heart ready to hear it, is one of the most penetrating pieces of Scripture we have been given. What was the psalmist thinking when he wrote "Where can I go from your spirit?" (verse 7). His understanding of God was that God knew everything about him. There was no place nor time in which the writer could be "just by himself." God is there and knows him—and us—completely.

It was important for the Jewish readers to understand that faith concept—that God knows us completely. That concept meant that the keeping of the Torah, or Law, required more than just going through the motions of acting good and dotting the i's and crossing the t's in their lives. If it were true that God knew them completely, then God also knew the motivation behind their keeping of the Law. God knew their hearts. A faithful Jew was to keep the Law not so much to avoid a penalty if he broke it (like a speeding ticket), but because in the keeping of the Law, the relationship between God and the chosen people was strengthened and deepened. Since God knows my very deepest heart's thoughts, there is no use for me to try to hide anything from God. I keep the Law because God knows me.

The faithful Jew, however, still had the freedom of choice at every step of his or her life. The choice to sin or to be righteous before God was an option every time the Jew acted, spoke, or thought. If this were not true, then there would be no need to worry about keeping the Law, to worship, or to strive to live faithfully. In that case, God would choose who would do all of these things and when they would do it. We would just "be along for the ride." We would go through the motions of an already lived out life.

In that context, then, we look at the portion of Scripture for today's lesson and can talk about the issue of predetermination in our lives. The psalmist talks with God, and says,

- God is a creator God: "I am fearfully and wonderfully made."
- God is an all-knowing God: "Your eyes beheld my unformed substance."
- God even knows all the days of his life: "In your book were written all the days that were formed for me."
- Yet, God is the mysterious One: "How weighty to me are your thoughts, O God! How vast is the sum of them!"

It is easy to see that the psalmist is more concerned with describing God and God's actions than he is in describing us and our lives. The psalmist's focus is not on what some persons have read to describe our "predetermined" existence.

The only thing the psalmist says here about predetermination is that all the of days of our lives have been formed. That idea really speaks about God's continual creation and about God's responsibility for each new day that comes into being. We are creations of God, "fearfully and wonderfully made." Our task is to live each of those days as the gift that they are from the God who knows us so well. The point is not about God predetermining every part of our existence.

WORDS FOR OUR TIME

Imagine what it would be like if, indeed, all of our lives were predetermined. Every pain, injury, loss, death, disappointment, and heartbreak would be part of your life because

God placed it there. What type of a relationship do you think you would want to have with a God who acted that way?

Take it a step further. If your whole life were predetermined, then every achievement, every noble act or thought, every brave or self-sacrificing thing you would do would not be your choice. It would have been placed there by God. How much encouragement would there be for you to do anything loving, or to strive to become more in the likeness of Christ, if you knew it was all predetermined? What incentive would you have for trying to improve your life?

Let's go further. We would need, of course, to release everyone from jail or prison, since their actions were not their fault, but were predetermined. We would never need to take responsibility for any of our ways of living, talking, or even thinking, since it would all have been placed there before we were made.

Finally, we would need no faith. Every person's sin, every person's act of worship, or the growth of every person in his or her relationship with God would all have been predetermined. Even our acceptance of Christ as our Savior would be a "done deal," with nothing for us to say about it. God would not have children that would be made in the image of God. God would only have rag dolls to play with, not sons and daughters to commune with.

God does create our days, and God creates the opportunities for you and me to respond to God's creation and God's love in real, original, and self-determined ways. What makes our faith and our lives so very precious is that our actions have not been predetermined as to how we will live and love. At each moment of our lives, we may say yes or no to being part of God's will and hope for our world.

Of course, when we say yes, we please God, because we agree to live out that "fearful and wonderful" creation in the way in which it was intended. God's will, however, does not overwhelm us; it always leaves us with the sad option of turning away from God. We all have the opportunity to sin just as we have the opportunity to live holy lives.

That is why it makes more sense to talk about God's purpose for our lives. Purpose includes God's will and hope for how we live and how we use the gifts God has given us. *Purpose* makes more sense than talking about God's plan for our lives. *Plan* sounds as though God has it all mapped out, and we have no precious choice left.

Certainly your life and mine have a purpose. Life's excitement comes when you discover your purpose and agree to participate in God's will and hope for this world.

WORDS FOR MY LIFE

How does it feel to know that God knows you so well? That is the real truth of this psalm. God knows you. God has always known you, probably better than you know yourself. How does that feel?

It may feel like an invasion of privacy! After all, who gave God the right to, well, "poke a nose" into my very private thoughts, feelings, and life? There are some things about my life that perhaps I would rather not share with anyone else, even with God. Yet, God is there, at the core of our existence, and no matter where we go, there God is.

Maybe you are a little frightened by having God know you so well. I mean, there are some things about my life of which I am not proud or of which I am ashamed. To know that the God of the universe knows all of that . . . well, it is very uncomfortable, to say the least. I wish that I could paint a little better picture, a sort of facade between God and me. Let's have a pleasant and cordial relationship, but let's not get too personal.

It might be that you do not care that God knows you so well. My life is up to me, isn't it? In the end, I have to look myself in the mirror, and if who I am is not who I should be, well, then it does not matter if God knows or not. It is all in my hands.

A better, more faithful approach to knowing that God knows me so well is to remember honestly who I am. I am a human being, created and not Creator. God has made me. In the very making of me, God knows all of me. Even better, God loves me. God loves me enough to create the days of my life, the ability to laugh, cry, wonder, and even rage and fight. God loves me enough to take all of me, good and bad. God invites me to let go of the bad and grow in the good, which simply means becoming all that I can be as a child of God. God has called me into the very closest relationship possible that any created being can know. It is the core of my life, rooted in

God's love that has made me, redeemed me, and sustains me.

Each day is laid out before me, with the opportunity to choose to live in communion with God. It is not a predetermined path of life, but a wonderful journey that I and every other human are called to make.

My knowledge of God, however, is very limited, except in the ways God has chosen to reveal to me. Like the psalmist, however, I come to understand that it is not so necessary to know God completely, even if we could. Our minds and brains just are not made to be able to comprehend it all. It is more important to be known by God so fully that our tears, joys, hopes, and fears can be held by the One who holds us.

I think that is why God sent Jesus Christ. God knew our pain and our tendency to separate ourselves from God. With the gift of Christ—by his life, death, and resurrection—we are reconciled, as Paul says, once and for all with the God who has always known us. In Christ, we have the freedom to grow in our knowledge of what God intends for us. We also have the ability to know God just a bit more fully. In Christ, we see God's perfect love that has no bounds, not even the border of death itself.

How does it feel to know that such a God as this knows you? Honestly, it ought to feel magnificent.

7

What Does the Bible Teach About Wisdom?

Proverbs 9:1-12

The fear of the LORD is the beginning of
wisdom,
  and the knowledge of the Holy One is
insight.

Proverbs 9:10

WORDS FOR BIBLE TIMES

The Bible is full of references to wisdom and to wise persons. Of course, the most famous story about wisdom comes in the account of Solomon. During a dream one night, God offers King Solomon any single gift (riches, long life, power over his enemies). Solomon asks that he be granted the gift of wisdom. God grants him this gift, and Solomon receives all of the other gifts as well. Solomon reigns over Israel as long as he uses the wisdom given to him.

The Book of Proverbs is a book of "wise sayings." The Book of Proverbs describes both a wise person and a foolish person by their actions and their approach to the world. In places, the Book of Proverbs also talks about Wisdom itself as a personified being, or creation of God.

So what is wisdom, according to the Bible? Well, wisdom is not simply intelligence, quick thinking, shrewdness, craftiness, slyness, or any of those types of "mentally sharp" descriptions. Wisdom is also more than insight or good judgment, although both insight and good judgment seem to be benefits that a wise person receives.

The Book of Proverbs seems to say that wisdom is grown

from a way of life centered in God. "The fear of the LORD is the beginning of wisdom" (Proverbs 9:10). Wisdom is a quality of life and character that develops within a relationship a person has with God. The relationship includes an awareness of God's presence. With that relationship comes a reverence, awe, or "fear," which is a terribly clear understanding of who we are as human beings when we stand face to face with a holy and righteous God. This fear and reverence leads a person to a right understanding of who God is. This right understanding results in a desire to worship and adore God.

Scripture seems to assert that within the life of wisdom, then, we are given our true moral center. We focus on God with our thoughts and our decisions. As we live with God in our lives, we act with insight and understanding, which bring with them a sense of ethical and moral uprightness. The writer of Proverbs calls this a laying aside of immaturity and walking in the way of insight. Insight is another way for saying we discern the mind and will of God for our own lives.

The path of wisdom in the Bible is not meant to be a drudgery. In Proverbs 9, Wisdom takes on the personality of a woman who offers us a banquet, a feast for all who would come and take part. We are invited to eat and drink and to be served, as though living with Wisdom is a joy and an eagerly anticipated event.

The naming of Wisdom with a feminine voice follows the Hebrew practice of making otherwise hard-to-grasp concepts more real. In the Book of Proverbs, Wisdom is given a strong feminine image, to the point where "she" stands as a separate personality and participates in God's creation of the world (Proverbs 8:22-31).

This does not mean that Wisdom was seen by the Hebrews as a female god, anymore than the church as the "bride of Christ" is truly believed to be a female entity. It also does not mean that Folly (found later in Proverbs 9:13-18) is only and totally a woman. Endowing concepts with masculine or feminine qualities simply makes it easier for us to relate to them.

As someone follows that path of wisdom, then, and grows in relationship with God, the writer says that natural benefits of long life and strength are given. Living in wisdom creates more wisdom because as our relationship with God deepens and we live out that reverence and awe and high moral character, we become even more mature and wise.

WORDS FOR OUR TIME

Where is wisdom found today in our world? Most of the time when we think about wisdom, we tend to think of advisers, consultants, and the like in secular settings. "Wise people" are described more in terms of how knowledgeable they are on a particular subject, how shrewd they are, or how well they can "put a spin" on a particular situation. Is that wisdom?

We also have an image of "wise old" persons appearing as an owl or a guru sitting by himself on a mountaintop. With those images, "wisdom" becomes something mysterious and out of place in our world or something we have to leave the world in order to find.

Wisdom in today's world seems to be a scarce commodity. It often gets set aside to make room only for facts, figures, and interpretation. Fact and figures do not bring life to our lives, however. Wisdom is much more profound than simply knowledge. Wisdom is a gift that comes from living in the constant awareness of the presence of God. Wisdom for us as people of faith is a sacred matter, not a secular one. The pursuit of and growing in wisdom is a lot of work. It demands that we take on a particular way of living. It is sacred because it calls us into a relationship with God in which we become honest about who we are and aware of the power and glory of God. As I mentioned before, that is what is meant by the "fear of God."

Imagine what would happen if the leaders of our secular world gave themselves over to living out a sacred life of wisdom in devotion and awe of God. From the president to the Congress and Supreme Court, to all governors, state legislators, business and corporate executives, labor leaders, teachers, professors, social workers, military leaders, and others—think of what it would be like in our world if they all were living out a life of wisdom. How differently would they make decisions and set directions for their countries and enterprises? Imagine if we were under the rule of truly wise people. Even more, imagine if the lay leaders of our congregations all were men and women who were wise according to Proverbs. Would there be different decisions made about ministry and resources as a result? What would be the spirit of your church if you were always cared for by a truly wise pastor?

I expect that if wisdom were to play a larger role in our society and church, we would see all our leaders more in tune with and open to God's will for us. We might see a radical reorienting of our society's (and church's) priorities. We would probably spend our money differently, use our time differently, and approach problems and challenges that would come along in an entirely different way. There would probably be less conflict and more opportunities for discernment in the solving of problems.

This is not to say, of course, that we live in a country or a church devoid of wise people! Many persons have a deep commitment and faith in God that is readily reflected in their decisions and outlook on life. However, are they in the majority? How can we, as the followers of Christ and the sharers of faith help to grow and encourage the producing of wise people to lead our world?

WORDS FOR MY LIFE

Wisdom is not a short-course activity. It takes a lifetime of commitment to God. It requires a process of growing and maturing in faith. As the writer of Proverbs was quick to point out, the fear of the Lord is the beginning of wisdom, but it is only the beginning and not the entire transformational trip!

Again, *fear* does not mean here just a scared feeling. Nor is it a dread of God. It is the acute awareness of God in my life leading me to focus my attention and energy on God's will for me. After this kind of *fear* is part of my life, I need to begin to grow into a time of faith building, through study, prayer, and reaching out to others in the practice of God's love through my love.

Finally, I am ready to receive a fullness of spirit devoted to God. In the fullness of spirit, our words, thoughts, and actions reflect God's will and love for us and for the world in a clear and mirroring way. We come closer to the likeness of Christ. Perhaps the reason that a wise person is depicted as an older adult is because it may seem to take that much living to see the growing evidence of wisdom.

The old saying is that a little knowledge is a dangerous

thing. That makes sense to the extent that when we only know part of what we need to know in a certain situation, we may make a decision based on partial, relatively small knowledge. That little knowledge may mean we are led to make a bad decision.

A little wisdom, however, is not like a "little knowledge." Even if we only have a little wisdom, it is still a good thing. Even when we only partly offer our lives into God's hands, recognizing only partly who we are when placed in the light of God's holiness and love—even then, that bit of revelation concerning God and us will give us holy insight, which is wisdom. With that wisdom, we can change the world, at least in a small way.

8

Did Isaiah (and the Other Prophets) Know Jesus Christ Was Coming?

Isaiah 9:2-7

For a child has been born for us,
  a son given to us;
authority rests upon his shoulders;
  and he is named
Wonderful Counselor, Mighty God,
  Everlasting Father, Prince of Peace.

Isaiah 9:6

WORDS FOR BIBLE TIMES

Prophecy fulfills two specific roles in the books of the Old Testament:

- One type of prophecy tells the truth of the present, as when the prophets criticized the nation of Israel for its injustice and turning away from God. Prophecy in this sense holds up a mirror to a person or society and forces them to look at themselves and their need to repent.
- The second type of prophecy tells the promise of the future. Throughout the Old Testament prophets' books, and in parts of the New Testament, there are references to a future person, event, or time brought into existence by God for a particular purpose. In this case, the prophets were allowed to peek into the future and to communicate a promise from God to the people of God.

In our lesson for today, the prophet Isaiah talks about a time in the future when the people will "live in light." In that future time, their "burdens" and "oppression" will be lifted. How will all of this come about? "For a child has been born for us, / a son given to us."

The change that will occur will come because God will intervene by sending someone to free the people. It will be someone who is born into the role of world-changer ("child," "son"). He will have authority. He will act in justice. He will occupy the throne of David. His kingdom will be an everlasting kingdom. All this will happen because God will bring it about. This passage describes a messiah, a savior-king, who will free the people and rule by God's authority.

What a promise! The prophets believed that God would bring this about, just as surely as God brought freedom to the Israelites from Egypt and Babylonia. They believed it would happen at some time in the future. The only things that were not clear to the prophets were exactly who the "child" would be and when this marvelous event would happen.

We can assume from the prophecies, since they specifically talk about

- a child,
- the throne of David,
- for the Jewish nation,

that if they had known the information about specifically who and when, they would have written it.

The prophets knew and believed, however, that it would happen. The prophecy sometime and somewhere would be fulfilled. It was enough for them to have faith that God was in charge of history and could be entrusted with the future, even a future that included a messiah.

As we move ahead in time, then, to the birth, life, and death of Jesus, we can imagine the disciples and others in the early church. They had given their lives to following Christ and now were looking back to the writings of the prophets that spoke of a messiah. As they studied those prophecies, they began to understand and believe that the promise of the prophecies was fulfilled in Jesus Christ's life. In Matthew's Gospel especially, which seems to be written for a Jewish-Christian community, there are numerous mentions of prophecies and the way in which they become answered and met in Jesus' life. The early Christians were able to do what the prophets had not done—they put a name and a time to the answer of the prophecies.

WORDS FOR OUR TIME

Prophecy is different from fortune telling or reading fortune cookies. Prophecy is not "divination," nor peering into a crystal ball, nor astrology. Prophecy is the work of communicating God's intention and will for this world, both in the present and in the future. Sometimes, as was mentioned, the prophecy turns out to be a word of judgment on a present way of living that is contrary to a healthy and growing relationship with God. In those cases, both the offense and the means of overcoming that breach in the relationship is spelled out for those willing to listen.

Sometimes communicating God's future intention is not as clear. We are always given a future hope, and we are given the assurance that God is in charge of the future as God is in charge of the present, but the ways in which that future hope will be played out is always in God's hands. God does not need to spell out the specifics—what God requires is our trust.

The prophets definitely knew that Jesus was coming. They just did not know it would be Jesus. As we look back over the course of history and look at both the future-directed prophecies and the life and ministry of Jesus, it makes sense that Jesus was that future promise of God now with us. Jesus is the Christ, anointed and sent by God to reconcile humans to God and to bring freedom from our sin.

We need to understand, however, that even what makes sense to us is sensible only because we look at it through the eyes of faith. We have the benefit of two thousand years of Christian tradition.

During the time of Jesus' ministry, there were numbers of charismatic teachers and mystical leaders who also called themselves "messiah." Jesus was asked the question frequently, "Are you the Messiah?" This was not because the entire society believed that Jesus was the Messiah, but because many others already had made the same claim. Indeed, Jesus' death in

Jerusalem came in part because the claim of "Messiah" and "Son of God" was more than the religious community's leaders could handle.

Not everyone today is interested in believing that Jesus fulfilled the prophecies laid out centuries before he was born. The Jewish faith community, for example, still "waits for the Messiah" and does not accept the Christian faith claim that the Messiah has already come. Indeed, among those who try to claim the Christian faith are sects and groups who discount Jesus' fulfillment as the prophetic Messiah.

One of the means by which we come to understand who God is and what God intends for us both today and in the future is the study of the Scripture. As a matter of faith, we as Christians can believe that the Gospels are indeed accurate and true as they hold Jesus up to the template of prophetic history and declare that he is the Messiah.

WORDS FOR MY LIFE

What does it mean for us to say that Jesus is the Messiah, the One whom the Old Testament prophets said would come into the world, free Israel from foreign domination, and establish the throne of King David for all time? After all, most of those prophecies appear to deal with the life and future of the particular Jewish faith community. I have never been Jewish—are the prophecies then just a part of Jewish history? Do they have meaning for Christian faith today?

As I think about the prophecy of Isaiah and reflect on the title of Jesus as Messiah, I consider that the prophecy is important for both the Jewish community at the time and for our lives today. I believe that God has the power to fulfill prophecy far beyond even the imagination of the prophets. The prophets did an excellent job of calling the Jewish community to hope and anticipation, which gave them the strength to go on even in times of exile and oppression. Jesus came, however, not only to be the "Savior-King" for the Jews, but for all humankind—even for me today. Jesus' power to extend God's mercy, forgiveness, and grace to every woman, man, and child is for me an exciting and awesome proof of just how much God loves us.

What is unknown to us as Christians today? What of God's will and hope for our world has yet to be made fully known to our church, to our spiritual leaders?

One of the things that allows the Christian faith to be a lively and growing faith is the understanding that God's revelation to the world was not simply a long-time-ago affair. Granted, we believe that God's fullest revelation has come in Jesus Christ. We hold that truth at the core of understanding our faith. However, we do not know the exact time and situation for when Christ will come again. We only know that his coming is promised. We do not know completely God's specific will for the body of Christ or for our own lives today. We only know that Christ called us to "preach the gospel" and to teach and baptize throughout the world. The particular ways in which that happens in our own communities and lives are not clearly laid out. Seeking God's revelation for our lives and for our world is one of the great works of our faith. We are called to study, to pray, to learn, and to discern that will—in a sense, to understand God's prophetic call to our lives in our time, so that the powerful and true prophecy of Christ's coming may be proclaimed to each generation and "every living creature."

9

How Perfect
Do I Need to Be?

Matthew 5:48

"Be perfect, therefore, as your heavenly
Father is perfect."

Matthew 5:48

WORDS FOR BIBLE TIMES

The Sermon on the Mount is a favorite portion of Scripture
for many persons. As you ponder this verse from the
Sermon on the Mount, keep in mind the audience. Matthew
5:1-2 says, ". . . after he sat down, his disciples came to him.
Then he began to speak, and taught them, saying. . . ." There
may have been crowds of folks on the mountain, but Jesus'
sermon is for his close followers. In it, he lays out a way of
life for these disciples. His words, then, are for those who
have committed themselves to following him.

Beginning with the Beatitudes, Jesus gives his disciples the
image of being salt and light to the world. In part, this means
that there is a higher, more holy standard of behavior and
ordering of life that they are called to assume because they
follow Christ.

We can really only read Matthew 5:48 in this context.
Verses 43 through 47 serve as a prologue. Jesus uses the word
therefore in verse 48, meaning that the verse relies on what
came before it to make sense.

Verses 43-47 talk about love. Specifically, this passage talks
about love of enemies. If the disciples wish to follow Jesus,
they must go beyond the limit of the law that called for one
to love the neighbor while it permitted one to hate enemies.

Disciples are to offer the love that God has given them without restrictions, even to those who persecute them! Otherwise, they are only doing what everyone else does—even the Gentiles. That is honestly no great achievement. However, intentionally to love someone who hates you is a great and awesome thing.

Disciples are called to offer a sacrificial, holy love. It gives without the slightest expectation that there would be anything in return. It is a love that redeems. It is both strong and gentle in the face of those who would answer with hate and evil. In fact, this love that disciples are called to offer both enemies and neighbors is a love that fully reflects God's love. It fulfills and completes the law, even though a strict understanding of the law would allow them to use their love selectively.

This highest level of love is perfect love. Perfect love so reflects a sense of the holy that it is the love that God offers to the world. It is a perfect love, as God's love is perfect.

Have you ever thought of perfection in those terms before? Normally, we think of perfection as "making no mistakes" or a "perfect 10." The idea of being called by Jesus to be perfect in that way surely would have sent the disciples (and us) scurrying away. But that does not appear to be what Jesus meant. When we read in the Bible, for instance, that Abraham or Job were "blameless" or "righteous," it does not mean that they never sinned. What it means is that they fulfilled the requirements of the law in terms of sacrifice and repentance. They were brought daily back into a relationship with God. Perfection is not a static, once-and-for-all state that we achieve—it is a dynamic relationship with God, in which we love and reflect God's love for us.

WORDS FOR OUR TIME

Even setting aside the concept of perfection as "no mistakes," this way of perfection is still a great deal of work. It requires energy, devotion, and singleness of heart for perfect love to become part of one's life. Even harder, we always live in tension with our neighbors and our enemies as we try to offer perfect love. Jesus never says that we can be perfect all on our own. We can only show that perfect love of God as we are in relationships with other, often imperfect human beings.

That is hard for me. We can find lots of reasons not to love others. We have seen an incredible increase in communication through the Internet and other media. We can talk about a global community, but for many of us, our circle of friends and significant relationships is much smaller than those enjoyed by our grandparents. They knew and cared for whole communities and neighborhoods. How well do you even know, much less love, the family that lives two blocks away? In our world, it is not so much a "love versus hate" option— as in love neighbor and hate enemy—as it is a matter of loving a few people that we know and finding ourselves not really caring about the rest.

Yet those people beyond our intimate circle remain. Christ's call to us to live as disciples means that we are called to take on the world, so to speak, with the love of God that is perfect and self-giving. Perfect love is the goal of all Christians. I should say, "perfect love" should be our goal, for if it isn't, then what goal do we have? What less-than-complete devotion to God and to Jesus Christ do we assume if it is not what Christ has called us to do?

We need to hear a word of grace in all this. We tend to feel as though we are faith-failures when we do not love the whole world perfectly. It is important to place this command of Jesus in the framework of spiritual growth. As we live our lives in relationship with Christ, our lives are not just static and idle. We grow in our faith. We move toward a living out of all sorts of aspects of a life in Christ. One of those aspects is loving others in a perfect and holy way. You see, perfect love is not an achievement. It is a way of life that we take on. We strive to live in a dynamic, growing relationship with others that comes out of our relationship with God. We do not "do" perfect love—we live it.

WORDS FOR MY LIFE

I play the banjo. That is, I received a banjo as a Christmas present twenty years ago when I was in college. Once or twice a year over the past twenty years, I have taken the banjo out of its case, tuned it, and played "You get a line and I'll get a pole, we'll go down to the crawdad hole." It's my greatest hit. It's my only hit. You see, over the past twenty years, I have managed to hold my skill on the banjo at the same level, which is the first page of the first lesson in the book. The fact is, I actually just own a banjo. It's out in the garage right now. I do not really play it—I just sort of play with it.

Unfortunately, in my life sometimes I "just sort of play with" the calling to live in perfect love. Even worse, sometimes I just leave it in the garage. I find myself loving discriminately, the way the world loves. By my actions I fall into the decision that I would rather just live as someone with good manners and minimal interaction with the world, than to live as a disciple of Jesus Christ.

"Be perfect, therefore, as your heavenly Father is perfect." Jesus does not give us the option of "try" or "give it your best effort." We do not have the choice to "do it when things are convenient" when it comes to a life of faith and a life of love. The word is BE. Assume in your life that this is your only option—to love both neighbors and enemies, which includes everyone. Yes, it is a matter of growing in the spiritual life to realize that fully by our actions and our hearts, but the command remains. The ideal and goal are still out in front of us.

"But no one can be perfect! Just Jesus!" Again, if by perfection you mean never making a mistake or error, then you are correct. However, as we look at our lives of faith, perfection is a journey we take. We begin by refraining from doing evil—just obeying the law. We move to doing good and loving acts. Then we proceed on to intending in our hearts to do loving acts. Finally we live a life of holy love, in which every response and reaction we make is one of love after the example of Christ. That is our goal.

10

What Is the Sin That Can Never Be Forgiven?

Matthew 12:31-32

*"*W**hoever speaks against the Holy Spirit will not be forgiven, either in this age or in the age to come."**
Matthew 12:32

WORDS FOR BIBLE TIMES

J esus cured a man who had been blind and mute. The Scripture says that a demon caused these afflictions. After Jesus cured the man by casting out the demon, the Pharisees spoke among themselves and accused Jesus of being in league with Beelzebul, "the ruler of the demons." They claimed that only by demonic power could Jesus have healed the man. In response, Jesus argued that Satan would not cast out Satan. Indeed, Jesus caused the miracle by the Spirit of God as proof that the kingdom of God had come.

Jesus then offered a warning about the "unforgivable sin." The sin that Jesus talked about is not simply blasphemy against God, nor against the Son of God; it is blasphemy against the Holy Spirit.

The word *blaspheme* means to impugn or to malign the work of God. Instead of saying, "Here is God's hand at work in the world," a blasphemer would say, "This cannot possibly be the work of God; God cannot do these things." In effect, Jesus accuses the Pharisees of slandering the work of God. They see the miracle performed, and say in so many words, "God has not acted here."

Are words enough, however, to bring down a judgment of

eternal unforgivenness? After all, Jesus says, "Whoever speaks a word against the Son of Man will be forgiven." That person may have not received a revelation that Jesus is indeed the Christ and could be forgiven for ignorance.

For sinning against the Holy Spirit of God, however, there is a different penalty. To say that God's Holy Spirit does not, cannot, or will not act in this world implies that God is powerless, or that something else could be greater than God. That is certainly a serious accusation! But is it serious enough to prevent someone from receiving the gift of God's grace and forgiveness?

First, we need to understand that the people of the New Testament time took the work of the Spirit and spirits seriously. To say that a healing could come about only because an evil spirit acted, and not because God's Spirit chose to bring healing, would definitely speak against the power and love of God.

We can look at Jesus' words in terms of a way of life. Imagine if someone were to say only one time in her life, "I believe in God." In every other moment before and after that, she said there was no God. Would you honestly believe she was in a relationship with God? No. By her persistent behavior, speech, and denial, she would stand and live apart from God.

When we look at the sin of blasphemy, then, we can view the sin in terms of a life path. More than simply a moment of speaking against God's power and presence, someone decides to live a life separated from God. He defames the Spirit of God in our world. At every opportunity, he shuns God's love and grace, God's healing and power. He consistently and persistently speaks ill of the presence of God in the world. He either says God does not exist or says God is impotent in the face of the world's power.

At the end of his life, after his death, it would only naturally follow that God would take that person at his word, that he chose to have nothing to do with God. The result? An unending separation from God—unforgivable sin. It is a horrible state of existence, and yet it is precisely what the person asked for.

WORDS FOR OUR TIME

We need to take the Holy Spirit of God seriously. The Old and New Testaments understood that God actively intervened in creative, redeeming, and sustaining ways, both in the lives of the faithful and in the world at large.

Our present time, however, offers scientific explanations for why things happen. We tend to be preoccupied with physical things. We are "immune" to the signs of God's presence and influence in the world. To be sure, we have made incredible discoveries in the areas of medicine and natural sciences. Yet even these findings cannot explain all of the happenings in our world.

Faith can explain some happenings, however, as we look at our lives from the perspective that God is at work. God moves among us, nudging, healing, and creating every day. God is also a freeing and redeeming God, who sometimes does things in a miraculous way! God promises to act this way; we should expect and anticipate that God will act to bring a greater peace and abundance to our living. God's Spirit will empower us to create, redeem, and sustain others in justice, peace, forgiveness, and healing.

We can, however, ignore it all. Unfortunately, we can even worship at church and only hear self-help sermons that make us feel better for the moment; we may not open our eyes to the presence of God. We ought not to ignore God, take God for granted, or even act as though God is just "Someone out there in the great somewhere." We ought to actively point out and share the signs of God's presence and loving action with one another so that our faith will be further strengthened. When we anticipate God's presence, our hearts are ready to experience it.

If we spend our lives only "getting by" in the world, limiting ourselves only to what we can see, touch, taste, or hear, then how are we any better off than someone who actively denies the presence and work of God in this world?

WORDS FOR MY LIFE

Blasphemy is different from questioning our faith. One can read this passage from Matthew and feel as though any questioning or struggling with God's work and power in the world is tantamount to blasphemy. But to mature as a follower of Christ, sometimes we are led on our journey of growth to question, inquire, even doubt and struggle as we try to discern God's activity and will. To pray sincerely "My God, my God, why have you forsaken me?" could be construed as blasphemy if we were to interpret it rigidly as God's unwillingness or inability to act on our behalf.

Our faith is more dynamic than that. There are times when we feel very close to God. We are attuned to God's work and leading. We know that God is in charge and will act to bring a new creation, to bring a full redemption, and to sustain us. There are times, however, as we face a crisis or a time of "walking through the valley of the shadow" when we may feel set apart and isolated from the God who brings us life. Both of those ways are faithful. We struggle and grow in our spiritual life in the presence of God's Holy Spirit, but it is a dynamic and moving relationship. It is more like a tree that grows, instead of a building that is built.

Blasphemy is an entirely different way of acting and living. The word is used to describe someone who consciously spurns God's activity in this world by the Holy Spirit, who hardens himself or herself against God's grace and forgiveness, and who simply shows contempt for God. Sadly enough, you may know persons in your community who fit this description. I know that I do.

Important: our role as Christians in an often non-Christian world is NOT to count and to identify blasphemers. Our task as the children of God is continually to hold up the evidence of God's love and action to a doubting and "blaspheming" world. We are given the task of proclaiming the good news, of preaching the gospel, and that does not include judging others' faith or nonfaith.

11

Did God Forsake Jesus on the Cross?

Mark 15:33-37

At three o'clock Jesus cried out with a loud voice, "Eloi, Eloi, lema sabachthani?" which means, "My God, my God, why have you forsaken me?"

Mark 15:34

WORDS FOR BIBLE TIMES

Mark does not mention any other words Jesus spoke in the hearing of those persons standing at the foot of the cross. By three in the afternoon, Jesus had been nailed to the cross for six hours. It was a horrible, painful, terrifying time. Suspended by his outstretched arms, when his legs grew tired of pushing up his body so he could breathe Jesus would begin slowly to asphyxiate.

After six hours on the cross, Jesus cried out, "My God, my God, why have you forsaken me?" Soon afterward, he died. Some persons standing close by and listening thought that Jesus had tried to summon the prophet Elijah as a savior to release Jesus from his place on the cross.

Readers have often argued the question that is the focus of our lesson: "Did God forsake Jesus on the cross?" Some would say that God did turn away from Jesus in his time of crucifixion. They believe that as Jesus became the remedy for the sin of the world, his sacrifice gathered up all of the sin of humankind and it was placed on his shoulders. At that moment, God in God's holiness could not look upon such sin, and so some believe that God did "forsake" the sin that Jesus carried.

Others say that no, God did not forsake Jesus. However, in Jesus' pain and agony it felt as though God were an entire universe away. Jesus went through the pain and humiliation of a public execution. After six hours, his spirit was so broken and hurting that he came to believe at that moment that God had left him to die alone.

Both these ways of thinking have existed for a long time in our faith history. In many respects both have merit. However, a careful look at the Scripture of the Old Testament can give us a new insight.

Jesus loved to quote Scripture. He did so as he went through the time of temptation in the wilderness of Judah. He quoted it when he spoke to the gathered worshipers in Nazareth. He used it when dealing with the question of what the greatest commandment would be. Now Jesus is on the cross, suffering and dying. Is there any reason to think he would abandon his love of Scripture at that moment?

Jesus quoted Psalm 22, which begins with the same powerfully intense words:

My God, my God, why have you forsaken me?
Why are you so far from helping me,
from the words of my groaning?

The psalm, coming just before the Twenty-third Psalm, is a prayer asking for God to save the petitioner from suffering, pain, and attack on his or her life. At this point of Jesus' life, with death imminent, he returns to the Scripture for hope and release from pain. He quotes Psalm 22 because its verses express how he feels at this moment of his life.

Jesus felt pain, loneliness, and maybe even fear. His use of "My God, my God, why" was not a word of challenge, however. Nor did it arise from a lack of faith. Jesus must have known the entire psalm, which ends with words of faith, comfort, and hope:

He did not hide his face from me,
but heard when I cried to him (verse 24).

We can imagine that as Jesus died, these words brought him closer to God, rather than expressing desperation and hopelessness. Even in his death, Jesus spoke words of faith in the God who did not let him go, even on the cross.

WORDS FOR OUR TIME

A couple of years ago, our church began the practice of including the words of the Lord's Prayer and the Doxology as part of our worship bulletin. Why? About two years ago, a mother and daughter came into my office expressing their appreciation for the worship service the previous Sunday. They then asked, "Where can we find that one thing we said after you prayed? You know, the saying that goes 'Give us bread,' or something like that." They were talking about the Lord's Prayer. They were adult women and had never memorized nor learned the Lord's Prayer.

When I thought about the thousands of times I have prayed the Lord's Prayer, or recited the Twenty-third Psalm or some other piece of Scripture without any hesitation, I received a real eye-opener that there would be even one person who would not know these familiar words. We now place the words to the Lord's Prayer in the bulletin for every worship experience I lead.

How easy it is for us twentieth-century Christians to assume Jesus had either lost faith or was being rejected by God on the cross as he spoke the words, "Eloi, Eloi, lema sabachthani?" We assume that out of ignorance. We do not readily know today what words and phrases were considered holy and faith-producing by first-century Jews. Perhaps in our churches and other faith communities, we should examine those words and phrases that we take and speak for granted so that when strangers to our traditions come to join us, they will not feel as though they really do not know what we are talking about, either.

We do not live in a "Christian," "churched" society anymore. Persons and families view the life of worship and church work as an option. As I write this lesson, I am preparing for a Christmas Eve service. We can expect two or three times the number of persons to come to worship that evening than on a regular Sunday. What is their experience of worship and of devotion to God when they only come once or twice a year? The church is in danger of losing that vital link of tradition that carries the power of the Lord's Prayer, the Twenty-third Psalm, John 3:16, and Psalm 22 into a new generation. When that is lost, then folks simply come to know about the Christ, instead of knowing Jesus Christ in their lives. It is a matter of faith, and faith is always tied to learning and growth.

How well does your church welcome, inspire, and educate the strangers to the faith. In the next century, will there be faithful persons to continue to spread the message of the gospel?

WORDS FOR MY LIFE

After seeing the movie, *Mary Poppins*, the word, *supercalifragilisticexpialidocious* became for many persons a great word to use when they did not know what words to say. The word did not really catch on in modern language as an idiom, but it sort of makes sense. There are simply times when we are befuddled, or in pain, or "at a loss for words." At such times a ready-made word or phrase can come to the rescue and fill in the gaps. I tend to believe that the reason persons curse and use vulgarisms is that they lack imagination.

In our faith lives, however, it is good to develop and use an expanding body of prayer and Scripture that becomes a vehicle for linking our hearts to God's. Have you ever been in such pain and hurt that you just did not know what to say to God? "The LORD is my shepherd . . ." Have you ever been filled with such joy and hope that you felt as though you could not even express it?

Bless the LORD, O my soul,
and all that is in me,
bless his holy name (Psalm 103:1).

By using these traditional, ancient words, we open the depth of our lives to communication with the Spirit of God. Instead of having to try to find "new words," these words are sufficient to tell God our pain or joy.

Paul wrote in Romans 8: "We do not know how to pray as we ought, but that very Spirit intercedes with sighs too deep for words. And God, who searches the heart, knows what is the mind of the Spirit" (verses 26-27). Paul understood that a spiritual life means much more than simply what happens physically.

Sometimes, our spirits are so burdened down or so confused that to speak a prayer out loud would almost trivialize our pain and our struggle. It is at that point that we are offered the promise of simply opening our hearts to God, perhaps through the reciting of a prayer or a Scripture verse that scratches the surface of our troubles. So long as our hearts and souls are open to God, God through the Spirit hears whatever prayer we offer.

This is what Jesus did on the cross. "My God, my God, why?" were words that became a sigh too deep for words. Jesus could barely breathe and was racked with pain. Nonetheless, out of the resources of his faith life, he found the prayer of Psalm 22. Instead of abandoning or rejecting Jesus, God's grace and powerful love sustained Jesus even to death so that we might be reconciled with God through the gift of Christ's life. If God would care for the Son of God in such a powerful way, we can surely believe that God will care for us in our time of "sighing."

12

What Happened in the Transfiguration of Jesus?

Luke 9:28-36

While he was praying, the appearance of his face changed, and his clothes became dazzling white. Suddenly they saw two men, Moses and Elijah, talking to him. They appeared in glory and were speaking of his departure.

Luke 9:29-31

WORDS FOR BIBLE TIMES

God works in mysterious ways. The reason God's works are mysterious is because often they are not limited to normal, ordinary human goings-on. That can make things uncomfortable for us because we like to know, understand, and explain all things as though we have all knowledge of the workings of the universe and beyond. A good example of an uncomfortable happening is our troublesome Bible passage for this session: the story of the transfiguration of Jesus.

Jesus is in the region of Galilee—in the city of Bethsaida—north of the lake. He has fed the five thousand with five loaves and two fishes. Then he has spent time with his disciples, asking them "Who do you say that I am?" Peter responds that Jesus is the Messiah of God. Jesus then talks about the suffering and death that he must endure. He calls the disciples to take up their own crosses and to follow him—to lose their lives for his sake, so that they will find them.

About a week after that conversation, Jesus follows his normal pattern of activity and goes off to pray and be alone for a time. He decides to go up on a mountain, probably Mount Tabor. He takes Peter, James, and John with him.

Luke then describes what the three disciples must have witnessed on the Mount. While Jesus is praying, something happens. Luke writes that Jesus' appearance changes. It is "dazzling." Two men appear in the same dazzling form and talk with Jesus. They are Moses and Elijah, and they talk about what Jesus must go through in Jerusalem, with his death and the bringing of salvation to the world. Notice in the Scripture that the disciples, though terribly sleepy, are able to see this event. Peter, always ready to jump into things, offers to make three dwellings—one each for Jesus, Moses, and Elijah. He likely has the idea that they all will just stay up on this mountaintop and enjoy the heavenly view.

Suddenly, in a way reminiscent of the baptism of Jesus, a cloud appears. A voice speaks the same words as at Jesus' baptism, that Jesus is indeed God's son and God's chosen. When it all disappears, Jesus is left alone with the disciples.

So, what happened?

It appears that the Transfiguration is more for the benefit of the disciples than it is for Jesus. The voice, which in Jesus' baptism, says, "*You are* my beloved Son," states in this instance, "*This is* my Son," and directs the disciples to listen to him. The disciples are astounded to find with Jesus two of their greatest heroes: Moses, who represents the foundation of the Law, and Elijah, who represents the foundation of their prophetic tradition. These two from Israel's past link the community of faith with the eternal kingdom that will come as a result of Jesus' ministry.

The disciples are so dumbfounded and terrified that they are content, at least for the time, to keep their peace and say nothing to the others about what has happened. But they are not alone; others have had an "epiphany" experience. Moses met God in the burning bush and later on Mount Sinai. Paul encountered Christ on the road to Damascus and was blinded by a bright light. Even at the tomb on Easter morning, there was a mysterious, unexplainable appearance of "two men in dazzling clothes" (Luke 24:4). All we can say is that God brought these things about.

The disciples were honored guests at an event that was to help Jesus do what he needed to do. In a sense, just as Jesus fed the five thousand hungry people a short time earlier, so in the Transfiguration he, as the Son of God, was fed and strengthened. In any reading of the Scripture, it is important to keep focused on the truth of the event and not try to explain away the things that cannot be explained very well in our human limitations.

WORDS FOR OUR TIME

What value is there in our study of the Transfiguration? It depends on what part of the story we are examining. If we consider the supernatural aspects of the story, it may give us an opportunity to think about the imagery used in the Bible to describe the glory of God. The disciples had not seen anything like this before. All they could do was to use descriptions that sounded other-worldly or to recall the Old Testament imagery of dazzling whiteness and heavenly clouds.

The only problem with that approach is that we rarely, if ever, are given similar experiences in our faith lives today. Our visual experiences of God tend to be limited. They often are held suspect in the light of scientific method and theory. We talk about miracles as special saving events, but not usually events in which we see dazzling light or other heavenly visions. To base our understanding of the Transfiguration on these images may lead us to a frustrated wishing that we would be able to get that same type of unusual vision for ourselves.

Think for a moment, however, what it would mean for us to study this story in terms of what God has done! In a moment of prayer and devotion, committed totally to listening and communing with God, Jesus was visited and strengthened for the heartbreaking mission ahead for him. His disciples witness this godly visit and gain a glimpse of "heaven." They must also have gained a tremendous sense of power for their own ministry. That is a powerful miracle of God! It stands as a great event in the life of Jesus whether or not the specific supernatural details are included.

What freedom and opportunity to grow in faith we have when we are able to think about the Transfiguration in terms of God's willingness to strengthen us for the ministry and tasks ahead for us as well. From this point in the New

Testament story, to the appearances of Jesus following the Resurrection, to the Day of Pentecost and elsewhere, God encourages the people of God to get on with the great work of living as witnesses to the faith in Christ that brings hope to this world.

For us as living disciples today, this is the gift of the story of the Transfiguration.

WORDS FOR MY LIFE

Have you ever seen God? Have you ever seen Jesus?

Some persons today believe they have been given that gift of a personal visual revelation of Christ. Sometimes what accompanies such a revelation is the strength and peace to do powerfully loving and holy work in this world at a particular time in their lives. Those persons live in an aura of spiritual strength. When we hear the stories of their experience, we are strengthened for the tasks ahead of us as well. Think about the devotional books you have read or testimonies you have heard that talk about God's revelation to someone.

Most of us, however, are not so blessed. I cannot honestly say that I have "seen Jesus" face to face in my own life. I have no deeply spiritual account that I can share concerning a revelation of God to me. The closest I can come to such a revelation is to look in the eyes of my wife and my two children, and to see their love for me, and their beauty of spirit and holiness that is a gift of God to me. I do know and believe that they are in my life by the hand of God. My "miracles" come in the lives of those who have touched me with God's grace and peace.

A miracle is nothing more nor less than the in-breaking of God's love and power in this world. Sometimes it happens through what we normally call miraculous occurrences, but it is not limited in any way to those supernatural events. It occurs any time our lives are blessed with the assurance of God's love. Who first told you about Jesus Christ? Who offered you love and acceptance and perhaps even forgiveness in Christ's name at some point in your life when you desperately needed it? Who called or invited you into a new way of living as a child of God and a follower of Jesus Christ?

I was amazed a couple of years ago when a long-time

friend of mine wrote me to tell me that I had been one of the reasons for his coming to a life of faith in Christ! I had done nothing unusual or "holy" around him in all of the years we have known each other. He explained that he came to see Christ in me, and he wanted that presence of Christ for his life as well. I was humbled and brought to prayer, and I gained the understanding that God can miraculously use us to appear to others.

Tell me then: How have you lived as a miracle to others? How have you allowed God's love and power to break-in to the lives of those you meet and live with? Understanding miracles and vision this way, it is a blessing to see how God acts in holy and extraordinary ways even in ordinary lives like ours.

13

How Much Faith Is Enough?

Luke 17:5-6

"**I**f you had faith the size of a mustard seed, you could say to this mulberry tree, 'Be uprooted and planted in the sea,' and it would obey you."

Luke 17:6

WORDS FOR BIBLE TIMES

Jesus treated different folks differently. This is not to say that he was bigoted or discriminatory. Rather he expected different standards of faith and behavior for some groups than others. For example, Jesus criticized the Pharisees so greatly because he expected them to know and to live out the highest level of faithful Judaism. When they did not, Jesus poured out his wrath on them.

Another group for whom Jesus had high expectations were the disciples. Often, however, the disciples failed to meet those expectations. In Luke's Gospel (17:4), Jesus talks about forgiveness and the way in which his disciples are to treat one another. He holds them to a high standard of behavior and lifestyle. The disciples listen to Jesus' words, and it must appear a bit overwhelming; so they ask him to "increase our faith!" They apparently believed Jesus could empower them somehow to do the holy and loving things that he called them to do.

Jesus responds with what should be a word of hope and grace, not only for the original disciples, but for us. He uses the famous "mustard seed" analogy to talk about the tremendous resource of faith available to us. "If you had faith the size of a mustard seed . . ." Jesus says, you could perform the incredible tasks of faith and forgiveness that are so needed in this world.

A mustard seed is one of the tiniest seeds we could find on earth. It is about one-twentieth the size of a kernel of corn. You could easily hold a hundred or more mustard seeds in the palm of your hand. It is small enough to be eaten whole by birds or blown aloft in a strong wind. This tiny seed, however, is amazing in its potential.

Mustard plants in the Middle East are different from the mustard plants we know in the United States. Where we grow mustard plants that can be harvested like a row crop with a combine, mustard plants in Israel can grow to be the size of small trees. Perhaps if Jesus were on earth today in America, he would have used the analogy of a tiny acorn and a mighty oak. The point Jesus wanted to make was that the growth from such small seeds is almost beyond our comprehension.

With this comparison, Jesus tried to say to his disciples that the work of doing God's will in this world is not limited only to those who are giants in the faith. You do not need the faith of Samuel or Elijah to accomplish what God has set before you. Granted, those faithful saints were great examples for the disciples and others of how life could be lived in relationship with God. However, just the faith the size of a mustard seed can do incredible things—like uprooting trees, if that were necessary.

Did Jesus, then, tell the disciples by this object lesson that they were lacking in their faith? I do not think so. These were followers who had been with him from the beginning of his ministry, selected by him. They were people who had walked away from the life they knew to walk with Jesus instead. That took some real faith in itself.

Moreover, the disciples' faith must have grown and matured over the course of their daily contact with Jesus. The fact is that the type of living Jesus was calling them to act out was difficult. They wanted more strength than they believed they had. I think Jesus wanted them to see that the faith they already had—as small and insignificant as it appeared to them—was enough to do the fundamental work of forgiving, loving, and serving God in the world. You do not need the greatest faith, Jesus seems to say. You simply need the faith that will act. A little, tiny faith, when linked with God's power, can accomplish miraculous things.

WORDS FOR OUR TIME

Mother Teresa undoubtedly will go down in twentieth-century Christian history as a true saint of the church and a giant of faith. Her ability to care in Christ's name for the poor of India leaves us close to awe. We say to ourselves, "I could never take on such a role." What is critical for us to discover as Christians is that we are not called to take on the role of anyone else in this world. Instead we need to realize what it is that God calls us to do in our own world, our own time, and our own relationships.

The mustard seed faith ought to be a core image for understanding our spiritual growth. Do you hear the good news in Jesus' words? By God's grace, you do not have to be Mother Teresa in order to make a difference in the world. By God's grace, you do not have to be the finest teacher, the most excellent preacher, the greatest healer, the best steward. There is nothing wrong in all these. If you are gifted in this way or others to serve God and to minister to the world around you, then consider that a blessing. It is not, however, a prerequisite for an abundant life in Christ. What Christ wants is our availability.

We need to remind ourselves that God's work in this world will be accomplished because God chooses it to be done. Our sole effort in ministry—a word that simply means "serving"—is to be ready and willing to be used by God. Great faith, marvelous abilities, and tremendous courage are wonderful. But Jesus says if you only have a tiny, little, almost invisible faith, yet are willing to use it, then miracles will indeed happen in your life.

This is a radical understanding of our cooperation with God. Today's Scripture tells us that our prime responsibility is to use what God has given us, since faith is always a gift. God will then empower that faith in ways beyond our imagination. Once again we will be left in awe of what God has done. I expect if we were to interview

Mother Teresa, she would say the same thing about her own life.

Today's lesson also says something about who we are. Our tendency even as Christians may be to discount or belittle our own faith, much like the disciples did. We may tend to say, "Oh, I could never do such things in my own life—that would require more faith than I have!" as if we have a manual somewhere that tells us what amount of faith is needed to accomplish each particular task in this world in Christ's name.

Maybe we say that because we do not have confidence in our ability. We think if we had "more power" we could do the work of God more easily. It could also be that we may be giving ourselves excuses for why we are not doing God's will more consistently and strongly in our lives. "I just do not have enough faith," and God says "Yes, you do—you just do not know it or want to admit it."

WORDS FOR MY LIFE

What is it that God wants you to do in your life? Do you have enough faith to accomplish it? If not, how much more faith do you need, and how do you go about getting it? These questions probably should be the first questions we ask ourselves every morning as we rise. What does God want me to do this day?

The most important and potentially far-reaching discipline we can develop as Christians is to be able to focus intentionally on the question of how God wants to use our lives. Too often we go through life and build in some "taking for granted" types of activities: we go to church most every Sunday, we give money, we may serve on a committee, we may attend a Sunday school class, we may be nice to our neighbors, and we may even let someone go ahead of us at a four-way stop. Are we intentional about doing more than that? Do we believe that we have accomplished God's will in this world because we are simply good church members? Think of how powerful the impact would be on this world if just a tithe—ten percent—of all Christians lived everyday with the question, "What does God want me to do?" and not the question, "Well, what should I do with my life?"

When we are able to discern God's will, we are able to live more faithfully with the issue of whether we have enough faith to do the work we are called to do. How much faith is needed becomes something we can offer back to God. With a daily guiding question of being open to God's leading, we are able to see better all our world as an opportunity to be in ministry in Christ's name. In our work or schooling, in our homes, our leisure activities, and elsewhere, we can see that what we do in our lives is only the means by which we share God's love. Our faith by a natural course will grow, and will indeed be enough to meet the task. As we recognize this, let our prayer move away from "Increase our faith," to "Open our eyes so that we may see Christ wherever we are."

14

Where Is the Kingdom of God?

Luke 17:20-21

"**F**or, in fact, the kingdom of God is among you."

Luke 17:21

WORDS FOR BIBLE TIMES

One of the great things about the Pharisees is that they frequently tried to engage Jesus in theological discussion. Granted, the reason for the discussion was often so that they could use his answers as ammunition against him. They wanted to show him to be a false prophet or someone who did not deserve to be taken seriously. We benefit from these discussions because they give us the opportunity to look deeper into Jesus' words about those important theological issues.

The kingdom of God was believed by most Jews to result from the coming of the Messiah, the savior-king who would set the people of Israel free and reestablish the throne of David that would last forever. They understood that although God created the earth and all that is in it, God's total and complete reign (which once existed in the garden of Eden) had not fully existed since the Fall. Sin and the actions of sinful humans had parted the world from full communion with God. With the coming of the Messiah, however, a new era in history would be brought into being. All humans would know God and would gladly live under God's rule then and forever.

The Pharisees were teachers of the Law. Some of them

asked Jesus the question: "When is the kingdom of God coming?" This question was both complex and sinister. It implied that Jesus should know when the Messiah would come. Would Jesus tell the Pharisees that he was the Messiah himself? To do so would surely bring charges of blasphemy or sedition against him. He would be seen as a dangerous individual. Whoever spoke the words, "I am the Messiah," had better be ready to back up the words with a revolution against the forces of Rome. If Jesus claimed that he was the Messiah, Rome would execute him for sedition and treason. On the other hand, if Jesus were to say, "I don't know when the kingdom of God is coming," his base of support and following would be eroded. Many followers who hoped Jesus was the Messiah would leave for someone else who would accept the mantle of messiah. The Pharisees were shrewd opponents to place Jesus between two traps.

Jesus' answer to the Pharisees was neither what they expected nor was it what they hoped for. He did not answer the question the way the Pharisees asked it. Jesus reframed their question. He shifted the definition of the kingdom of God from a political entity to a way of being and living before God.

What then, did Jesus say? He told the Pharisees (and us) that the kingdom of God comes mysteriously—as mysteriously as every other creation of God. "The kingdom of God is not coming with things that can be observed," he said. Where the Pharisees liked to pride themselves on their insight into the acts and will of God, Jesus jabs their pride by noting the absurdity of saying, "Look, here it is!" God's kingdom instead already exists among the listeners of Jesus.

This was a bold statement made by Jesus. He said that God's complete and eternal reign was already coming into being. The kingdom was coming into being without a military or political takeover. It was coming into being as God reestablished a relationship with God's people graciously and lovingly. It was coming into being as Jesus Christ himself lived among the people. It was coming into being as people saw God in the flesh.

The kingdom of God was not a future, only-hoped-for event. It had already come. It was growing and becoming revealed to everyone who encountered Jesus. The kingdom of God would be made known in a powerful and sure way to the followers of Christ both in the moment of his crucifixion and death and in the sunrise of his resurrection. God is in charge, and God reigns. As the "Hallelujah Chorus" states, "The kingdom of this world is become the kingdom of our Lord and of his Christ."

WORDS FOR OUR TIME

"Where is the kingdom of God?" It is amazing how captivated with the physical and tangible we human beings are sometimes. We want to put our finger on the place of God's rule! Isn't it interesting that the Pharisees were busy asking, "When is the kingdom?" but Jesus answered with "where." Now that we are asking, "Where?" it may be that we need the answer to the question, "How is the kingdom of God?"

The kingdom of God—defined as God's authoritative, overarching rule—has already come to this world in Jesus Christ. God is definitely in charge of the workings of this world. God has once and for all reclaimed the world as God's own through the grace of Jesus Christ. This is what we believe as Christians—not that Christ has just saved me or us, but that he has brought about a radical reordering of the world's life. Through the gift of Jesus' life, death and sin have been rendered impotent when we look at them from the viewpoint of eternity and God's power.

Wait a minute, now! If the kingdom of God is already here, and if it exists throughout the world, not limited by any other governmental body or religious group, why then is the world not at total peace and harmony? Why does it seem in so many places that God is powerless in the face of evil actions by individuals, groups, governments, and nations?

It is at this point that the how of God's kingdom needs to be explained. Just as Jesus came and changed the world forever without taking over a single government or fighting a single war, so God's kingdom is coming fully into being today, sometimes in hidden ways. If we believe that the relationship between the world and God has changed forever by Jesus' gracious life and his death on the cross, if we believe that God and we have been reconciled, then there is no more war or battle to be fought. That is why Jesus, in giving the Great Commission, did not say "Go into all the world and take it over, battling for control!" Instead, he commanded the disciples to preach the gospel—that is, to simply tell the good news of what has already occurred by God's hand. In due time, the world will come to know fully God's grace, as each heart is changed and healed from the separation we have had from God through the centuries.

God's kingdom is here, and it is coming to be known fully as you and I tell the story. God's kingdom grows as we invite others to join us under that joyful and peaceful love of God we know through Jesus Christ.

WORDS FOR MY LIFE

When I was a student at the University of North Dakota several years ago, I was studying one cold winter evening. Suddenly a friend of mine came barging into the room and shouted, "Come on, grab your coat! You have to see this!" I begrudgingly got ready and went outside into the subzero Dakota night. My friend was standing in the middle of the parking lot. He motioned me over, and said, "Now, look straight up into the air." I did, and saw one of the most spectacular displays of the northern lights that I have ever seen. They swirled with both green and red colors and looked like a bursting star. It was absolutely breathtaking. I had almost missed it. I had been busy inside my room with my nose in a book, consumed with what I needed to get done. It took somebody else to call my attention, to get me to look in a different direction, in order to see an unforgettable sight.

I am sure you can draw the analogy. In our very midst, the kingdom of God has come. How many times have we been oblivious to the presence of God's rule because we have had our own things to do? How many of us have locked ourselves away and are missing the abundant, just, peaceful, and loving existence brought by God's kingdom? Just because we do not see God's rule clearly sometimes, just because others have chosen to live in rebellion against God's reign, does not mean God's kingdom does not exist. It exists everywhere on earth.

Those who are loyal to God must become more irresistible, like a college friend who has seen something marvelous. We must share the good news as easily as we share other great things that have come into our lives. When we eat at a great restaurant, see a great movie, or read a great book, we are so willing to share with others what we have experienced. Then why, when it comes to our faith, are we afraid that we will be seen as pushy if we invite others to participate in the present kingdom of God? Perhaps we need to become captivated, not merely content, with what we have found to be true. We need to live in awe of God's grace alive and working through Jesus Christ. Then we need intentionally to share what we have experienced. That is how the kingdom of God is manifested in this world—one heart at a time.

15

How Much Should I Give to the Church?

Luke 21:1-4

He said, "Truly I tell you, this poor widow has put in more than all of them; for all of them have contributed out of their abundance, but she out of her poverty has put in all she had to live on."

Luke 21:3-4

WORDS FOR BIBLE TIMES

The Temple in Jerusalem was the central place of worship for the nation of Israel. Certainly there were other meeting places (which later became synagogues after the destruction of the Temple in A.D. 70), but when it was time to worship with sacrifices, gifts, and offerings, the Temple was the place to be.

The Temple had a treasury to provide for the upkeep of the buildings, to pay for the living costs of the Levites and the priests who served there, and to maintain the organization and the life of the Temple activities on a regular basis. There was no set fee charged to persons who came to the Temple, but it was expected that a gift would be brought. The traditional gift was a tithe, or ten percent of a person's earnings.

Note that people coming to the Temple did not come to bring gifts for the priests and Levites. They came to bring gifts to God. How those gifts were used by the stewards of the Temple was not an issue. The Temple belonged to God. The people of Israel found their center of worship in the Temple. Therefore, a gift was a natural consequence of that relationship of people and worship.

As Jesus watched in the Temple one day, he noticed persons bringing their gifts for the treasury. (By the way, most pastors feel a bit uncomfortable sitting and watching folks bring their offerings—but not Jesus!) The rich members of Jerusalem society naturally brought their gifts, which were received without much comment. Jesus then noticed a poor widow bring her gift. She put in two copper coins—traditionally, it is reported she put in two "mites," which were completely insignificant in terms of the overall value of offerings to the Temple that day. They were, however, of great significance for the widow—and for Jesus.

Jesus saw the widow's gift and proclaimed that her gift was the greatest of all gifts that day. Why? Others gave from their body of wealth—from their abundance—but the widow put in all that she had.

To be a widow in the society of Jesus' time was one of the worst possible positions. Women were generally viewed as belonging to their husbands. Women held little or no property rights or financial rights. Therefore, when a woman was widowed, she was forced to depend on her husband's brother (if there were one) or on her children for her livelihood. Widows were given the leftovers of society. When there were no leftovers, they received nothing.

Yet, this widow, totally dependent on others for survival, gave away all that she had. Jesus saw that and called hers the greatest gift. The widow's gift was an act of worship without reserve. The fact that it was such a small gift when compared to others was not an issue.

What Jesus says through this example is that the widow gave herself totally in worship to God. She now was completely dependent on God for her very life. She emptied herself, something that the others did not or could not do. That became a blessing to her from Jesus. Her story is told today as a result.

The most significant thing to remember about this story is that the widow did not give an offering to the church—she gave her all to God.

WORDS FOR OUR TIME

"How much should I give to the church?"

That is an interesting question. To answer it, you need to look carefully at your church's annual budget—how much it costs to maintain and run the building, pay the staff, retire the debt, fund the program ministry, and support the work of the denomination you belong to. After you total up all those needs, also including any special restricted benevolent giving you may wish to do (and do not forget to buy a poinsettia for Christmas and a lily for Easter!), you then should look at your financial position and see what available money you have after your other obligations are met. Based on all of that, you should have a reasonable figure that you can pledge or give outright to the church.

All of that, of course, is totally unbiblical. It is also completely unchristian and absolutely unfaithful as well.

I have told my congregation more than once not to give to the church unless for some reason they really want to make a contribution. Never, ever, ever give your offering to the church. Instead, give your offering to God.

"How much should I give to God?" Now that is a question that will turn our lives upside down—or right side up, as the case might be. When I determine what I will give in terms of what I should give to God, then I must ask myself what do I truly own. Can I say that I own anything at all? All that I have and possess right now in my life has come as a gift from God. My ability to earn a living, to feed my family, to do all and have all of those niceties of life are a result of God's blessing to me. I own none of this. When I die, everything physical I control in this life will belong to someone else. The phrase "you can't take it with you" is really a stewardship concept.

Everything that I now have gathered around me is only placed in my charge. It is only my responsibility for now. I am only a manager, a steward of that which God has entrusted me for the time being. Isn't it, then, arrogant to consider how much of God's things I should give to God? As we make our offerings, we should do so understanding that we are only placing the management of God's possessions from our hands into the hands of someone else. All is God's anyway, from start to finish.

The widow must have understood that. She must have known that the two coins were God's already. She was just transferring them to someone else's care in God's Temple. Imagine if our offering pattern as Christians were based on the clear understanding that what is "ours" is only God's. We are but caretakers of creation in all of its many forms, from money to everything else that surrounds us. We would be free to offer generously in thanksgiving for God's blessings, knowing that God will continue to care for us. The tithe as a biblical standard of giving becomes only a minimally reasonable standard when we realize that the other ninety percent of everything is also God's.

The church is placed in the position of managing God's things. As the body of Christ, it should be a good steward. The church uses those "things of God" to increase the ministry of Christ in the world and to spread further the good news of God's kingdom in accordance with Christ's commission. It is terribly unfortunate as well as a breach of faith and integrity whenever the church, as a manager of God's gifts, fails to be the best steward possible.

Our giving, however, should not reflect the efficient and effective productivity of the church. It should reflect our relationship with God. If indeed we do not feel that the church is the place to receive the gifts God has first placed in our care, then we should either give it somewhere else, or work to improve and repair the church's stewardship.

WORDS FOR MY LIFE

Money is not the issue. Our stewardship within the context of our relationship with God is the central issue of this lesson. In fact, just as the widow's gift meant something much more than two copper coins, so our gifts in support of the church's ministry are only symbols of something much greater. The church will always need money. We know that. There are always electric bills and salaries to pay, something is broken, candles are to be lit in the sanctuary, and so on. We live in a society that functions with money as a medium for exchange of products. The church must therefore use money. In fact, it is not an issue of lack of faith to say the church should not need any money—it is a lack of common sense.

God does not want your money, though. God wants you. God wants all of you, from the first thought in your head in the morning, to every word that you speak, to every effort that you make, to every gift that you give. God wants your heart, soul, mind, and strength. God wants your love. True stewardship understands that our lives are best lived when they are used to bring glory to God through everything that we do, say, and think.

Stewardship is a matter of making only one gift. It is the gift of your entire life for God's use. The widow's gift in the Temple was a natural consequence of a lifetime of giving the same gift over and over. Her life, like ours, has true value only when it is given away. This continual offering of our lives requires a measure of faith, however, and a willingness to live full time as a child of God. It is difficult to give ourselves away if we do not have the faith that God will continue to care for us and give us far beyond what we need to live. Offerings that are given out of fear and not gratitude are horrible things. As we grow in our faith, we come to depend on God for everything we are, and we live with every response as a response of gratitude for what God continues to bring into our lives.

In the church I serve, members are asked to "uphold the church" by their prayer, their presence, their gifts, and their service. This covers actions (service), possessions (gifts), intention (presence), and spiritual life (prayer). Even then, what we give to the church is only the gifts that we have first received from God. Our lives and the greatest gift, eternal life in Christ, are gifts we can never outgive.

16

Are Christians Really Supposed to Share All Their Possessions?

Acts 4:32-37

Now the whole group of those who believed were of one heart and soul, and no one claimed private ownership of any possessions, but everything they owned was held in common.

Acts 4:32

WORDS FOR BIBLE TIMES

What an incredible time to be a Christian! Only a matter of weeks after Jesus' death and resurrection, the disciples were living in Jerusalem. Pentecost had already occurred. The Holy Spirit of God filled the disciples' house and lives with power and assurance that allowed them to preach and teach a new message. Their message became: "Jesus Christ has risen from the dead, and has become the bringer of salvation and the Lord of the universe."

Thousands of people had already heard that message. These hearers had begun to follow the disciples, devoting their entire lives to faith in Christ. There was a closeness and an intimacy among the believers. One of the firm understandings was that Jesus would return to them soon. They were in a short waiting time, and they built their lives around that expectation.

It was a special time in the Christian faith. Scripture says that the believers were "of one heart and soul." They had no idea of creating a "church organization." They were a family. They preached and lived waiting for the head of the family to return. In this context, then, it only made sense that they would offer up everything that they had for the common good. Personal possessions would not mean much as soon as Jesus came again. The love they shared allowed them to give all and only take what each one needed. Even houses and land were sold. The proceeds were placed into the care of the disciples for distribution. No one had any need. In this way of living, the early gathering of Christians received great power and grace.

What happened? Something definitely did happen, because even later in the New Testament, Paul and other writers are silent about holding everything in common. Later writers are careful to say that Christians must share, but there is no word of giving up what you own for the sake of the whole.

It appears that at some time after the period described in Acts 4, the "experiment" of communal living ended for the early Christians. Perhaps they realized that the imminent return of Jesus would not occur as quickly as they thought. Perhaps their numbers grew so large and spread geographically so wide that it became impossible as an organization to hold everything in common. Perhaps new followers decided not to give what they had. Giving up all of one's possessions had never been a requirement of faith. It was simply something that had occurred. Outside of small sects or groups, such as certain monasteries or small communes, the concept of common holdings does not exist within Christianity today.

Was it all a failure? I do not think so. It was an important stage in the life of the early Christians and spoke strongly of their faith and trust not only in Christ's return but also in the care of their lives and their ability to give.

WORDS FOR OUR TIME

Imagine receiving a letter in the coming week from your pastor that reads something like this:

Dear Members,
    I have decided, as your spiritual leader, to invoke the biblical model set up in Acts 4. Next Sunday, I request

that you bring the titles to all of your homes, land, businesses, cars, investments, jewelry, collections, and everything else that you presently own. At the same time, any of you who have any debts or financial needs, please bring those in writing.

Following worship, I will redistribute the resources of our congregation according to the needs of each person and family. Since we are all good Christians, this should not be a problem to anyone.

Please also make arrangements with your bank and place of work to send all your paychecks and dividends to me. I will give you what you need to live.

I am excited about this new model for ministry! See you in church!

Your Pastor

Next Sunday would be an interesting day, right? Some folks might well take your pastor up on his or her offer. Others would either begin looking immediately for a new church—or a new pastor. Why would this new model not quite work out? Well, partly, it does not seem fair to most of us. We feel that someone who has been successful and worked very hard in life should not be required to give all of that away and only receive an allowance. Granted, we should take care of those in need, but it should come out of our own need to give and to share and not as a church membership requirement.

Another reason it would not work out is that we value our ownership of possessions. As we live in a material world, we find comfort and reassurance in the gathering of things around us. Most of us believe that what we have in our hands right now is what we own. Most of us do not see ourselves simply as stewards of what God has given to our care. We build walls of safekeeping around our things. We will be the ones to decide if we are going to share or if we are going to hoard.

The disciples of Acts 4 were living in the light of Christ's very-soon return. Possessions did not matter—only needs being met in the "meantime." What phrase would you use to describe the "light" that your congregation is living in right now?

Again, maybe it is a bit unfair to lay guilt on our congregations because we have not given all that we have into a common pot. That has not been the way of living that we

Christians have practiced for centuries. Even as stewards, we believe we are responsible for the things God has given us and that we ought not to simply hand it all away and become wards of the church.

Isn't it intriguing, though, to imagine our own congregations expecting Christ to return at any moment, and framing our ministry, our finances, and our love around that unshakable truth? The fact is, the time is closer than ever to Christ's coming again. We are living in the "meantime" ourselves. That should make a difference to us. No, we might not give all our possessions away, but we may as a congregation want to think about the use of those things placed in our care by God.

WORDS FOR MY LIFE

What keeps me from giving away all that I presently own?

First, I am scared. A lot of fear wells up as I think of not having anything. I fear for the future, for I was taught from an early age that you need to think about tomorrow's needs and to plan for them.

Second, I am satisfied with my present situation. I possess many nice things. I like to have them around me. They give me pleasure. I, like most Americans, like my "stuff." I am not eager in the least to let go of them without an awfully good reason.

Third, I think that spiritually speaking, I live more in the understanding of God's grace for me through Christ and Christ's teachings to love one another, and I live less in the faithful anticipation of Christ's momentary return. Therefore, I rarely share in a sacrificial manner, giving all I possess. My sharing comes more as a portion, as a token, leaving me with a comfortable cushion.

I see proof here of my need to grow in faith in God's abiding and sustaining love. I am sure that a spiritually mature person would have a much easier time separating him or herself from possessions and would understand that God has and will always provide.

It is also important to think about our trust in each other. The model of sharing in Acts 4 is a sharing among the followers of Christ. It is not a matter of giving all that we have away—it is a giving into the common care for each other. Perhaps I do not trust my congregation, or my friends and partners in Christ to take care of me. Or I do not trust them to use my hard-earned possessions "appropriately." Perhaps I have never tried, nor invited them to trust me, either.

The sharing of possessions among the early believers might not have to be our way of living. What we need for our own lives are hearts that trust, care, and share. Then we will be free to discern how God intends for us to use what God has given into our stewardship.

17

How Can I Be Worthy Enough to Receive Holy Communion?

1 Corinthians 11:17-34

For all who eat and drink without discerning the body, eat and drink judgment
against themselves.

1 Corinthians 11:29

WORDS FOR BIBLE TIMES

Corinth was an interesting church to serve. From Paul's letters to them, the Corinthian Christians sound like a bunch of hardheads. They squabble, fight, and bicker. It is a good thing none of our churches are that way!

The Corinthian Christians also had an interesting way of sharing in the Lord's Supper. They did not have Communion rails, brass containers, or crystal goblets. They did not have a sanctuary, for that matter. What they had was an instruction from Paul and a tradition of coming together to eat in the presence of Christ.

From what we read from Paul, Holy Communion for the Corinthians had become a picnic time. I wish we could say it was an early church potluck; but from the Scripture in 1 Corinthians 11, nobody shared anything with anyone. Paul is very critical of those who bring small banquets to the gathering, eating and getting drunk, while others go hungry.

This picture is of the gathered body of Christ sharing in Holy Communion—but no one is sharing. The poor are "humiliated," Paul says. The church is fractured and divided.

Within this context, Paul writes and gives the Corinthians "words of institution" for the sharing of their Communion meal. The Lord's Supper cannot be a time of gorging oneself while others sit starving. Paul presents them with a ritual and a reminder of the very heart of what believers should do when they take the meal. Instead of simply eating of the bread and drinking from the cup, believers are to recall that Christ said it was his body broken and his blood shed that established the new covenant with God. The believers are to remember and recall Christ with every bite they take. They participate in the death of Christ until Christ comes again.

That would certainly create a change in the understanding of that meal from an occasion for gorging and drinking.

Paul then warns the Corinthian Christians that if anyone comes to the table to share in the body and blood of Christ in an "unworthy manner"—with the idea of having a self-serving feast, not setting their minds on communion with Christ and with one another—then they can be assured that God will judge them.

Believers are to come to the table "discerning the body [of Christ]." They are to allow a sense of the holy and the awefull presence of God to sustain them until Christ comes again. Anything else is an "unworthy" manner.

Notice something unusual in all of this. Paul does not define "worthiness" the way that some folks might. To be "worthy" to participate in Communion does not require you be a member of a particular denomination; you are not required to pledge, give, or even be a nice person with a respectable job; you are not even required to stand up and make a public confession of your faith in order to be worthy to join in the meal. Paul's argument with the Corinthian Christians concerning worthiness was that they were so busy taking care of themselves that they turned the holy meal into a self-centered, self-serving time. By doing that, they neglected to come into the presence of the living Christ. They neglected to come ready to care for the person sitting right next to them.

WORDS FOR OUR TIME

Greg, a pastor partner that I work with in our local church, came back to the office simply furious from a visit he had made to the county jail. For a number of weeks he had been leading a worship service there on a fairly regular basis, offering prayer, guidance, and the sacrament of Holy Communion. It had been a meaningful experience for all persons involved.

He mentioned that, following each service, two ladies from the community would lead a Bible study for the inmates. The previous week, the Bible study leaders had observed the Communion service. They made a point later of asking the female inmates if they understood what they were doing in the Communion sacrament. The women had an idea about the worship, but did not have a crystal-clear, theologically firm explanation. In this sense, they may have been like many in our congregations.

Greg's anger came over something that happened the following week. The women who had offered Communion previously came to him with a concern. The Bible study leaders had said that because the women did not fully grasp the sacrament's meaning, that they were "drinking unto condemnation" and that it was a horrible thing. The leaders said that they should not have ever participated in the sacrament.

Can you imagine the arrogance? Here were women in jail, coming out of their own need to worship God, to find strength for their lives, and to receive God's grace in Jesus Christ. However, because they did not have the "right" understanding in their minds concerning the sacrament, they were "unworthy"! Greg's anger and frustration came from the fact that two self-professed Christian women—Bible study leaders—were so quickly willing to condemn, simply because the women inmates had not come up to the standards of worship understanding set by others.

First Corinthians 11, however, implies that an "unworthy manner" involves intent, not knowledge. The women prisoners intended to worship God and to receive the grace of Jesus Christ through the sacrament. Yet they were condemned by others for doing so. The Bible study leaders, in a sense, were feasting and gorging in their own faith, while allowing the inmates to starve in their faith. They actually took the food of Christ out of the mouths of the prisoners.

Who is unworthy?

WORDS FOR MY LIFE

The question for this lesson is "How can I be worthy enough to receive Holy Communion?" In one sense, we cannot be. We can never be. How can we be worthy enough on our own to earn the right to receive the body and blood of Jesus Christ? For us to try to achieve worthiness as though it were a standard of behavior or the completion of proper training means that we will always fall short of being acceptable Communion recipients.

That is not the issue in this Scripture passage, however. Nor is it the issue of the gospel. The fact is (we must remind ourselves), we are not worthy on our own to assume the role of equal partner with God. We have sinned—at least I have—and continue to do so even though Christ is part of our lives. I continue to come to Christ for forgiveness and reconciliation as an unworthy candidate on my own. I am unworthy, but I am also completely acceptable as someone who can be forgiven. It is by the grace of God in Christ that I have life and freedom. It is a complete and total gift to me. My worthiness, then, to live in Christ is also a gift. The invitation to come to the table and share in the meal Christ offers of himself also comes to me as a gift.

What is required of me to receive Communion is the same thing that is required of me in the whole business of salvation: I must be willing to receive what God offers me and to worship God with a grateful heart. This takes place not as though I deserve it. Nor have I accomplished it in any manner myself. The absolute freedom to come to Communion is a gift from the God who, through God's son, sets us a place. Our own worthiness is irrelevant. It's a matter of God's love that we come to this feast, just as it is a matter of God's love that we come into eternal life.

At the same time, God's grace is not cheap. We are called to continue to grow in that understanding of God's acceptance of us that brings us to a place at the table, even though we bring no food ourselves. Our Christian faith calls us to grow in gratitude for God's gift in Christ. We are called to share that gift as we are able. When we deepen our understanding of what it meant for Christ to die for us, the meal becomes dearer, sweeter, and even more filling for our hearts.

It is also true that we ought never to receive Communion as trivial or matter-of-course, especially if we know better. Like any act of worship, it is important that we prepare ourselves not just to enter the sanctuary but also to come into the presence of God. We offer ourselves in worship—and in Communion. We would be guilty of an "unworthy" manner of receiving the sacrament if we cared less whether we received it, or felt as though we are just going through the motions.

Worthiness for Holy Communion is a matter in my heart of coming as an honored guest. It is a matter of intent, desire, respect, and worship. It is a matter of the simple knowledge of God's love for me in Christ. That is, in the end, the core of worship itself.

18

How Important Is Belief in an Afterlife?

1 Corinthians 15:12-20

If for this life only we have hoped in Christ, we are of all people most to be pitied.

1 Corinthians 15:19

WORDS FOR BIBLE TIMES

Imagine yourself as one of the leaders of the new Christian faith in the first century after the birth of Christ. You have the sacred writings of the Hebrews and the Jewish Law. You have the eyewitness accounts of those who were with Jesus. You also have your own ability to reason. You do not have, however, any New Testament writings. Nor do you yet have any long-standing tradition within this infant faith.

It must have been an exciting time for Paul and the other early Christian leaders. They were responsible for discerning and explaining the truth of God's activity in Jesus Christ. As new congregations were established throughout the northern Mediterranean region among both Jewish and Gentile groups, ideas and beliefs were offered about who Jesus was. Some of these ideas differed from those held by the first apostles. Since Jesus had not spoken to the eyewitnesses about everything in his life and person, they had to sort out the beliefs of the new church from what they had experienced.

Apparently the Corinthian church was asking questions about the Resurrection. People held differences of opinion and belief not only concerning Jesus' resurrection but also concerning the general resurrection of all believers. By addressing some of these questions in his letter, Paul initiates the church's body of teaching about the Resurrection.

For Paul, the issue of resurrection was a matter of keeping trust and telling the truth. Did we tell you the truth when we first preached to you? If you do not believe all of what we said, but instead have decided to pick and choose pieces, then we are going to have some problems and the whole truth starts to crumble.

Was Christ resurrected? Well, let us go back to the issue of whether anyone can be resurrected. If all we have is this life here and now, with no hope of resurrection, then we have told lies to you and violated your trust: we told you God raised Christ. God could not do that if no resurrection is possible.

We have followed Christ. We have believed that we are freed from our sin. But we are still living in sin if Christ has not been raised. The Resurrection proves that it was not just a man named Jesus doing a noble, tragic thing and dying on the cross; instead, God's hand was at work in redeeming the world. God's resurrection of Jesus proves that God has power and authority. God is responsible for forgiving our sin.

If Christ has not been raised, then we are only talking about a nice teacher who was once alive but now is not. Our faith in the Son of God is "futile." Even worse, those who have already died in the Christian faith believing they would be resurrected have really just died. They have perished without hope. Worst yet of all, if with all the persecution and troubles we face, we only have this life and no eternal life, then we are pitiful. Life is indeed "nasty, brutish, and short."

Paul wants the Corinthians to realize that if they are going to believe in Christ as their Savior, then salvation rests in their belief in God's ability and willingness to resurrect Jesus and to resurrect all who trust in Jesus for eternal life.

Resurrection from the dead is critically important to Paul. In resurrection, God has broken the stranglehold of death, which is a natural consequence of sin. Therefore, forgiveness of sin is not just a matter of atonement and Christ's sacrifice on the cross. It is a matter tied to the very resurrection of Jesus Christ and to our new life in Christ. Because Christ died, we also have died to our sin. Because Christ is risen, we are also able to rise freed from our sin into new eternal life.

WORDS FOR OUR TIME

What difference does it make to us today to believe in the resurrection of the dead? For me, resurrection is one of the "legs" of our faith. As Christians, the first leg is that we believe some particular things about the person of Jesus Christ. He was the Son of God, the Savior of the world, the Messiah. He died on the cross outside of Jerusalem as a sacrifice for our sin, so that we might be reconciled to God once again. Jesus was resurrected after three days of death. Jesus, the Son of God, is the eternal Christ and the ruler of this universe and our lives.

A second leg of our faith comes in what God through Christ has done for us. We have been given a way of living through Christ's teaching and example. We have been given forgiveness for our sin. We have been invited to live a new life, enjoying a new relationship with God through Christ's death on the cross.

Both of those "legs of faith" deal with our present life. But resurrection moves us beyond just a present way of life. We find an abundant life in this one because we follow God's will in Christ. Resurrection, though, brings us into the realm of the eternal. Our resurrection propels us into the future. For all time and beyond all time, we will be with God. This life on earth is a wonderful gift, but it is only the beginning of an incredible existence in the love of God. Resurrection shows us just how deeply God loves us. God removes all barriers between us. In resurrection, we belong to God, not to death.

In our resurrection to come, and even as we anticipate it today, we move closer to God and away from fear. We are also invited to live beyond just what this life will bring to us. We leave self-centeredness behind, hopefully, and begin to pick up instead a life of love and self-giving. Resurrection empowers and brings courage to the call of Christ in us to live our lives following him. Resurrection brings freedom.

If we were to say that resurrection does not exist for us, then what is the most we can claim for our faith? God loves us, but only as long as we are on this earth. After we die this physical death, we are only a memorial gift. God forgives us for our sin, but when we die, our sin really will not be of any significance anyway, for death ends all that we are. We have limited the work of Jesus Christ to helping us live in a little better relationship with God on earth; but in the end it does not matter, for we still die.

You can see how trivial and minor the work of salvation becomes if resurrection is removed and all that we have is this earthly life. In fact, you can see how much less power God would have if, indeed, death spoke the final word. In that case, God could only stand by and watch. In resurrection, however, God brings us beyond and through the valley of the shadow of death, into the light of eternity. God is with us, and we are not alone.

WORDS FOR MY LIFE

My father's name was Roger William Cross. He was born in 1928 in Omaha, Nebraska. He had a career in the Air Force. He was married to my mother, Ruth, for forty-four years. Together, they had seven children. He was a good man, a moral, ethical person, although not perfect. He loved his church and his faith, his family and his friends. Dad died of cancer in July of 1993, when he was sixty-five years old.

Is it possible that the entire existence of this man was limited to only sixty-five years? Or that with all that he was, all that he did in his life, and all that he gave to God, that a disease would be more powerful than God's loving care of him? Does cancer, or a heart attack, or a car accident have more power than God? If so, then any of those acts of nature could render God a bystander.

That, of course, is not true. In Dad's entire life, he felt and shared the presence of God with him. He knew of God's love for him helping him through some difficult times in his life. God's love also helped him as he died to this life and was received into an eternal one. God's love was not limited in Dad's life; it brought him hope for the day and hope for eternity. I believe that Dad understands resurrection in a way more profound than I will know on this earth. I also believe that some day, as all of the children of God gather in an eternal time of peace and celebration, we will see each other again.

Why do you believe in eternal life?

19

What Is the Resurrection of the Body?

1 Corinthians 15:35-57

For this perishable body must put on imperishability, and this mortal body must put on immortality.

1 Corinthians 15:53

WORDS FOR BIBLE TIMES

Paul ends his first letter to the church in Corinth with a discussion about the future of all believers. He has already talked about the resurrection of Jesus and its significance. Now he explains what resurrection will be like for those persons who follow the resurrected Christ.

Resurrection is mysterious. Paul writes here not from observation or personal experience, not from a testimony of Scripture, not from a tradition of the yet-young Christian church. He writes in this place purely out of a revelation that God has given him.

What is the resurrection of the body?

Let us look first at what Paul says it is not. Our resurrection will not be only a resuscitation of the physical body. A giant cosmic defibrillator does not jump-start all our hearts. In fact, Paul rejects the idea of a resurrection into the precise physical form we occupy now, which he calls *perishable*, *weak*, and even *dishonored* when contrasted with the glory found in the resurrection body.

Nor will our resurrection be a general gathering of "spirit" out of our lives. Resurrection does not mean a releasing of all the positive, psychic energy in the world. Nor is resurrection a "ghost making." Our detached spirits will not drift around the world, inhabiting and haunting. Nor does Paul believe that our souls are only a little piece of God that returns to its origin after our death.

So, what is resurrection? Paul explains this new thing by using the image of a seed. A seed and the plant that evolves from the seed are two quite different entities. Paul says that God is the One who gives the plant its *body* that is so very different from the seed. In the death of our physical bodies at the close of our life on earth, God raises a new, spiritual, resurrected body. It is a qualitative change. Our resurrected bodies are "immortal" and "imperishable," freed from the limitations set by our presently frail physical life.

Note that Paul believes the resurrection of the body is not simply a natural consequence of life and death. God gives that resurrection. That new, spiritual body comes to us as a gift. The resurrection of the body expresses God's grace in Jesus Christ. Not only are we reconciled to God, not only are we given forgiveness of our sins, and not only do we gain eternal life with God, but we are also given the gift of a resurrected body—a body that is immortal and imperishable.

Please understand the context in which Paul is writing. The early Christians clearly believed that the return of Jesus and the general resurrection of the dead were moments away. The followers of Christ should prepare for this imminent event. All who had kept the faith would be raised and brought into a resurrected life to join Christ as he ushers in the new heaven and the new earth.

What is the purpose behind our resurrection? We do not receive it as a reward for good work done. God resurrects us so that God may be worshiped and glorified for all eternity by those who have been reconciled to God.

WORDS FOR OUR TIME

You and I will die sometime. Our physical bodies will cease to function. Our breathing and heartbeat will stop. Our brain activity will end. Is that all there is?

Scripture says no. As a person living in the faith in Jesus Christ, you are given a gift of eternal life with God. Death is not the "victor" in the battle for your life. Even with your earthly life over, your eternal life only begins. If that is so—and we believe it is—then what will that eternal life be like?

It is an honest question arising out of both faith and curiosity. It is probably a question that has led to many misconceptions being laid on top of, and perhaps getting in the way of, our faith:

- "When you die, you become an angel." (This notion is not scriptural—angels are the special creations who serve as God's messengers.)
- "If you are good, you go to heaven, and if you are bad you go to hell, which is run by the Devil with a pitchfork." (Nothing scriptural tells us that Satan is in charge of Hell or in charge of torturing evil people. Scripture does, however, mention judgment.)
- "When you die, you become a ghost, or a zombie, or some sort of 'spirit energy.' " (Again there is nothing scriptural about these notions.)
- "When you die, you are reincarnated into another life." (Reincarnation is not a Christian concept at all.)

The resurrection of the body that Paul describes in First Corinthians is so much greater than any of these. Eternal life is a quality of existence that can only be described as heavenly. A resurrection body is not something ethereal or vaporous. Jesus' resurrection body could be touched, fed, and recognized by his friends. Yet, the resurrected body is no longer bound to the struggles and pains of this earth in the way that our earthly bodies are. Paul describes a resurrected existence lived in joy and freedom and in the presence of God.

What a wonderful teaching for us Christians. We could not complain if God only gave us another day of life after our lives were over. Nor could we argue if God just removed the pain of this life and let us exist in a place of rest and peace. Instead, God brings us an even greater life than what we have today. God brings it to us with a body that meets the needs of an eternal life.

Is all of this a reward for our faith lived out on earth? Not really. Our faith in Christ should be its own reward. God does not give us special blessings because we decide to believe in Jesus. However, the promise of a resurrection body does give us the opportunity to praise God for all eternity. One of the old catechisms, or teaching tools about the faith, in the Christian church had as its first question "What is the chief end of [humanity]?" In other words, what is the main purpose for humanity's existence? The answer was, and still remains, "to glorify God." A resurrection body allows us to do without ceasing the work we have been created to do. In that, we have our greatest blessing.

WORDS FOR MY LIFE

Why talk about a resurrection body at all? What difference does resurrection make?

The answer is: hope.

As we look to the future, even to a future beyond our death, Christians are given the privilege of holding the profound hope that the future is in God's hands. That future is bright and filled with the powerful gift of eternal life and a resurrection body. Hope in that future gives us the strength to live for today with a long-range perspective. The struggles of our lives today—with bills, headaches, arguments, car wrecks, children not acting the way they should, illness, and everything else that makes life tough—all can be seen from the view of eternity. The things that overwhelm us in the short run and cause us to despair do not have the power to do that for long. We are able to look beyond our overwhelming problems to that hope in God's gifts to us. God assures us that God holds us throughout all the problems and trials.

Paul wrote in 1 Corinthians 15:58, just after the section of Scripture for this session: "Therefore, my beloved, be steadfast, immovable, always excelling in the work of the Lord, because you know that in the Lord your labor is not in vain." With resurrection hope, we are able to do an excellent work of sharing the gospel, seeking justice, healing, forgiving, and bringing peace and love to our world. As we live our lives in faith as the followers of Christ with the perspective of the eternal gifts God brings, we are truly given power to be people who know and share hope in its most precious form.

20

Should I Expect Ecstatic Experiences?

2 Corinthians 12:1-10

And I know that such a person—whether in the body or out of the body I do not know; God knows—was caught up into Paradise and heard things that are not to be told, that no mortal is permitted to repeat.

2 Corinthians 12:3-4

WORDS FOR BIBLE TIMES

Paul is boasting, and he admits it. Paul finds himself in the situation of defending himself to the church at Corinth, a congregation that he had founded. Some whom he calls "false apostles" had attacked him and his rights as the patriarch of the congregation.

You might want to read forward from Chapter 10 of Second Corinthians in order to understand the whole flow of Paul's argument. By the time you reach Chapter 12, you will find Paul talking about his own personal struggle in the Christian faith, especially his own sufferings and his special experiences of God's presence. He recites this list so that no Christian in Corinth will doubt that he is the premier apostle with the right to keep the charge of the congregation. The Corinthians should permit Paul to protect them from those who would lead them astray from the true faith.

So Paul boasts. He lists the numbers of times he was beaten, shipwrecked, imprisoned, attacked with stones, hungry, cold, and put in danger of all sorts. It seems like a strange accounting to make, but it is meant to silence any others who might think that their sufferings place them somehow in the same "league" with this apostle. Paul says that his boasting, however, is to show how God has worked in his life.

When we come to Chapter 12 in our reading for this lesson, Paul moves from boasting about his persecution to boasting of his spiritual experiences—what he calls the visions and revelations he has received from the Lord. The Christians in Corinth and the other places Paul preached certainly would have heard the story of Paul's conversion on the road to Damascus, when Jesus himself appeared to Paul (then known as Saul) and called him to a new life.

The other experiences Paul mentions are mysterious. Paul says they occurred about fourteen years before the time of this writing. He refers to "knowing a person" who had these visions, although in 12:7 he does refer to himself as that person. Paul uses the third person as a literary way of removing himself from too much boasting. He makes a point of reminding the Corinthians that he received a "thorn . . . in the flesh" to keep him from becoming too elated as a result of his visions.

What are these experiences? Paul talks about being "caught up to the third heaven" and being caught up to "Paradise." We are at a bit of a loss to understand what these experiences mean. This is the only reference to such things in the New Testament. The Old Testament does not help much either. In one Jewish tradition, there were seven levels of heaven (from which comes our phrase "she's in seventh heaven") with each higher level bringing a greater joy and bliss to the inhabitant. Another tradition stated that there were only three levels of heaven, in which case Paul would have been on the highest spiritual state of rapture and eternal joy. Using either image, Paul experienced some sort of spiritual, ecstatic occurrence that he considered a gift of God.

The visit to "Paradise" falls into the same category. Paul states that he is not sure whether his experience was "in the body or out." In other words, he is not sure if he had actually and physically visited this place or if he experienced a vision and revelation from God. He does know, however, that during that experience, he "heard things that are not to be told, that no mortal is permitted to repeat." Clearly, Paul believes that somehow he experienced heaven in a powerful experi-

94

ence while on earth. Note, however, that Paul believes that in order that he not become "too elated," he received a "thorn . . . in the flesh," which he also describes as a "messenger of Satan."

What curious and mysterious pronouncements! We need to remember, however, the purpose Paul has in even making these statements. Paul does not write them so that the Corinthians would be in awe and wonder over Paul's special spiritual power. Nor were they written so that the church members in Corinth would expect those types of ecstatic experiences for themselves. Paul's purpose is to prove to the Corinthians that his ministry and spiritual strength should neither be slighted nor ignored in his controversy with the "false apostles."

Note also that Paul clearly states that God alone has caused these mystical things to happen to him and that he is but the messenger and servant of God.

WORDS FOR OUR TIME

"Should I expect ecstatic experiences?" Should the strange, mystical, ecstatic experiences Paul evidently had be considered a part of the normal Christian faith life? If we answer yes, then should we not also say that all the different sufferings Paul listed in this context—stonings, floggings, shipwrecks, and so forth—should be considered a part of our normal faith experience as well? Should we not also expect some "thorn in the flesh" to keep us from becoming overly proud or satisfied, if we think Paul's experience is normative for what we as Christians should experience?

The Holy Spirit gives Christians a number of powerful, incredible, and faith-strengthening things. Paul, however, does not include "ecstatic or mystical experiences" as part of any list of the gifts of the Spirit. At the same time, though, we can look throughout Christian history and find accounts of the visions and special revelations persons of faith have received. Strange, mystical, spiritual occurrences seem to be an acceptable part of the Christian experience. Those occurrences usually have served to strengthen the recipient for special and sometimes difficult ministry. As we study Paul's own life, we can clearly see that his ecstatic experiences strengthened him in his faith and work.

We should not assume that all Christians will receive some sort of ecstatic experience. Some of us are not attuned spiritually to receive those types of visions or revelations. Some of us may be threatened or unwilling to experience that type of spiritual event. Others of us simply do not need such ecstatic incidents to strengthen our faith and relationship with God.

Others of us may indeed receive mysterious and rare gifts from God. Those are to be cherished and seen for what they are—gifts, and not badges of honor or privilege. In fact, those whom God blesses with ecstatic experiences may also be challenged with trials and persecutions for the faith.

WORDS FOR MY LIFE

My two older brothers and I always seemed to be arguing when we were growing up. I attributed those arguments to the fact that both of my brothers were so hardheaded. I was the only reasonable and insightful one. My mother might disagree with that statement. In any case, in our sibling rivalry we played a game that might be called, "Ultimate One-Up-Man-Ship." One of us would begin with a simple statement or assertion, and the other two would quickly claim something grander, greater, or more unbelievable. The topic did not matter: sports, food, accomplishments, goals, or the size of toad we saw in the backyard. The competition would usually end as one brother would say something so completely out of line that the other two would ridicule the statement and deny its truth.

Christians sometimes tend to play "Ultimate Spiritual One-Up-Man-Ship." We are not satisfied with striving to be a good, faithful follower of Christ; we insist on claiming to be the *best*, the most spiritual, and the closest-to-God Christian who has ever existed. It is a seductive and insidious game. It leads to a high level of smug, arrogant sin. We gloat that we have the best, the greatest, the deepest, the purest, or the liveliest of any Christians. Others are not nearly what they should or could be.

However, God gives us our capacity for faith. God gives

the gifts of the Spirit not for the glory and honor of the recipient, but so that we might do the will of Christ in this world. God sometimes even gives special, unusual experiences so that we might be equipped to do what God calls us to do.

In some ways, our reading of Paul's use of the word *boast* may be a bit off the mark. It is not a matter of boasting rights for us as Christians. It ought to be a matter of praise and thanks. We should boast about the awesome wonder that God would grant us such a relationship of faith and work to begin with. Our boasting is about God and what God has done.

"Ecstatic experiences," or any other type of spiritual gift, are to treasured and even feared. They are given into our stewardship of faith in order for us to become faithful and fearless in the life of the gospel.

21

How Inclusive Should the Church Be?

Galatians 3:23-29

There is no longer Jew or Greek, there is no longer slave or free, there is no longer male and female; for all of you are one in Christ Jesus.

Galatians 3:28

WORDS FOR BIBLE TIMES

Galatia—a region in the interior of present-day Turkey (known in Paul's time as Asia Minor)—was a melting pot for the new Christian church. Practicing Jews, former Jews, and a large number of Gentiles (non-Jews) attempted to blend together in the Christian congregations Paul had established. Paul's earlier preaching had been powerful and persuasive. The Christians of Galatia held a sincere devotion to Christ.

A problem arose, however, because many Jewish converts to Christianity wanted to continue with the dietary and levitical laws that had carried meaning and identity for them as Jews. Gentiles, however, had never observed such laws. Conflict arose over who was really worthy and righteous in the faith. Were Jewish-Christians who continue to observe the ritual practices of Judaism more faithful to Christ than Gentile Christians?

In his letter to the Galatian Christians, Paul sets before all Christians across the ages an understanding for freedom and equality in Christ.

Listen to the phrases Paul uses to describe the Galatians:

- You are all children of God through faith.
- There is no longer Jew or Greek.
- There is no longer slave or free.
- There is no longer male or female.
- You are all one in Christ Jesus.

A slave was property. Slaves did not deserve the treatment a free person would receive.

Women were second class, subservient, and without rights. Jewish men prayed a prayer that expressed their thanks to God that they had not been born as women.

Jewish Christians sometimes boasted they were better than Gentile or "Greek" Christians because they were part of the theological and faith history out of which Jesus had come. Jewish Christians had participated in a lifestyle of righteous living in obedience to the law since childhood.

The three categories of Greeks, slaves, and women were categories of lesser individuals.

Paul responds to this way of class division by saying no. If indeed, the grace and salvation offered by God in Jesus Christ only effectively and authentically comes to the individual by faith, then there can be no other prerequisites of righteousness that come by way of gender or accident of birth. "If you are clothed in Christ," and "one in Christ," as you profess, then there are no differences. No discriminations are possible within the body of Christ. The division of status must be set aside.

This statement must have been incredibly revolutionary. The Christian church must be a different model for the world's relationships. The church reflects God's grace active in the lives of the followers of Christ. The discriminations and divisions found in society are not allowed within the Christian community. They do not reflect God's grace.

Why would Paul stand against the norms of society in this way? Paul could have simply said that in this new Christian faith, Jews and Gentiles should get along and set aside their divisions. Why include slaves and women in the formula? Paul apparently had discerned Christ's intention that the world's way of seeing and treating people was inadequate. If Christ were indeed resurrected, it occurred for the whole world, not specific segments.

Paul's call for inclusion in the Christian community is a call for the total and complete sharing of God's grace, with no boundaries.

WORDS FOR OUR TIME

"How inclusive should the church be?"

I think that question is in some ways like the question the lawyer asked of Jesus, "Who is my neighbor?" To pose the latter question suggests that there are appropriately limits to the lawyer's neighborhood and to responsibility the lawyer has for another human being. To ask the former question about the proper extent of inclusiveness in the church established by Jesus Christ with his own sacrifice and God's grace belittles the salvation Christ brought.

The issue of inclusiveness has been settled. In God's kingdom, no quota systems are needed, no caucuses seek power for some or segregation for others, no subgroups jockey for position. The only title allowed is "child of God." God is not the least bit interested in the human differences we have identified and made important in our world. The scriptural phrases that best describe the extent of the church's inclusiveness are "for all have sinned" and "for God so loved the world." For us to have to ask the question of how inclusive the church should be is a clear signal that we have not yet come to understand God's love and God's gift of reconciliation through Jesus Christ.

The fact is, however, we still do ask that question. We still discriminate in all segments of our churches. Some of us have developed sophisticated "pecking orders" or privileges that come with position, tenure, gender, age, physical capability, or skin color. Some of us even pride ourselves when we manage partially to overcome those barriers so that there is a semblance of inclusion and oneness.

Even in denominations, we spend an incredible amount of time and money trying to legislate and develop programs that will create inclusiveness. It is very difficult to legislate and program a change of the heart, however. The necessary change, the transformation, the repentance, and the salvation must occur in the heart. We will never be an inclusive church as long as our hearts and minds are satisfied with leaving anyone out of the kingdom of God. Inclusiveness cannot exist in the presence of any wall that stands between two children of God.

Inclusiveness in the church needs also to go beyond the outer appearances and simple categories of discrimination. We need to examine the ways in which we subtly and quietly keep persons of all sorts from offering and using the gifts of the Spirit God has given into their care. Institutionally and personally, we are found guilty of impeding the work of the Holy Spirit in this world through inhospitable responses to others who come offering their lives. When was the last time you saw a person on the streets without a home as a person with God-given gifts to offer for ministry?

The only way that we will come to a true life of inclusiveness is by

- becoming aware of our sin
- repenting of that sin
- praying for a transformation of our hearts that then reflect Christ's heart

If, for some reason, we decide we do not want to be an inclusive church in all ways possible, then we must be prepared for Jesus Christ to set us aside. Christ will empower a new, more receptive group of persons to be the body of Christ.

What would an inclusive church look like? It would certainly not be monolithic. Inclusive means diverse, with different persons at different times leading, challenging, and teaching. It would be a church that would grow outward from the strength of treating people equitably. An inclusive church would call them all to live lives of holiness and service in the name of Christ. It would make use of the spiritual gift of hospitality, welcoming each person as a valuable and honored member of God's family, no matter how the world might discriminate. The only question that is asked is, "Do you know the grace of God?"

WORDS FOR MY LIFE

I spent the first two years of my elementary schooling at Amberly State School in Queensland, Australia. Every day, as school began, there would be a sea of little blue shirts and gray shorts, as the children came to class in the school uniform. There was something simple and yet profound about all that. It did not matter what family we came from, how tall we were, or anything else—when we came to school, we were clothed in a uniform that in many ways made our place in school equal with everyone else. I loved wearing that uniform, partly because it made me look like "the big kids." We all had at least that one thing in common.

I am not advocating school uniforms. I would rather see "church uniforms" to make us equal and bring inclusiveness to our Christian community.

The fact is, we have been given a church uniform. Maybe, though, we have decided to keep it in the closet. Paul says that we have been "clothed in Christ." Imagine if, in my life, the only thing that the world would see as distinctive about me would be that I was a baptized and faithful follower of Jesus Christ. How attractive that would be, as Christ's love and welcoming influence would show through me to the world that needs to be included in God's kingdom.

22

What Is the Antichrist?

1 John 2:18-25

Who is the liar but the one who denies
that Jesus is the Christ? This is the
antichrist, the one who denies the Father
and the Son.

1 John 2:22

WORDS FOR BIBLE TIMES

A fight for survival is going on. The persecutions of the
Christians have already begun. The forces of the Roman
Empire and others threaten to destroy the still relatively new
faith. But some others who have long been part of the
Christian community now try to change the way people
believe in Jesus. They even deny his divine nature and his
title of Son of God.

The writer of this letter of First John says, "[This] is the last
hour!" Holding firm to the belief that Christ's return to the
earth is only moments away, he describes the Christian way
of life as a battle of true faith and action against those who
would destroy, corrupt, or lie about the truth of Jesus Christ.
It is a time of great turmoil and struggle. Other letters and
books of the New Testament (as well as other early church
writings) reflect that sense of earthly and heavenly warfare.
The message has an urgency, a hard-edged concern that readers of the letter will soon lose their way. They may have
already lost their way and their place in eternal life with God.

The writer of First John talks about those who have set
themselves apart from the faith community: "They went out
from us, but they did not belong to us." At one time "they"
had lived within the structure, fellowship, and belief of the

faithful congregations. Now, however, they can only be called "antichrist." In fact, the writer refers to *antichrists* as a term for a whole group of persons who are acting and speaking a certain way. Literally, they are "against Christ."

What is "antichrist"? In verse 22, John clearly states "This is the antichrist, the one who denies the Father and the Son." There are persons acquainted with the Christian faith, maybe even who claim to be Christians, who are yet defined by their own statements that they do not believe Jesus is truly the Son of God. They deny Jesus is the Word made flesh, that he is the incarnation of God in this world. Because they deny the Son, John says, they also deny the Father, for the two are eternally linked.

The definition is simple. The truth of the gospel rests within the promise and hope of Jesus as the Savior, Messiah, and Son of God. If you believe that, then you follow the Christ. If you deny that truth of the faith, then you pick up the title of antichrist, "against Christ."

Please notice that the antichrist is not someone who simply does not know about Jesus Christ. Nor is it someone who has some hesitation of belief or some sense of doubt. Agnostics are not antichrists. The antichrist is someone who stands against Christ—it is intentional, decided, and total opposition to Christ. When we ask the question "What is unique about the Christian faith?" the answer must be "Christ." When that unique truth of Christ as Savior and Son of God is denied, there is no reason to connect with the Christian faith.

For the writer of First John, belief in Christ as the Son of God was indeed a matter of life and death. The antichrists needed to be identified for who they were. They have left the church community, but they continue to have a strong influence on those who remain. John warns firmly about that influence. "Let what you heard from the beginning abide in you."

Did you notice that the writer does not talk about Satan here? Nor does he mention a world ruler. Nor does he describe a political system like Rome as the antichrist. No, what this letter is concerned with is right belief. Right belief fashions one's faith and strength in the world. In the midst of a dark time of desperate struggle, in the last hour, true believers must avoid those who would destroy that faith. They must be wary of the antichrist, or antichrists.

WORDS FOR OUR TIME

Think for a moment about denying Christ. As good Christian folk, we would not dream of doing such a thing.

The kind of denial we are talking about here is, of course, different from Peter's denial in the courtyard that he knew Jesus. This is a denial that Jesus is the Son of God and the Savior of the world. Certainly we would never make that sort of denial.

We have the luxury of knowing the writings and thoughts of the members of the Christian faith over the last nineteen plus centuries. We have their experiences, their traditions, and even the Scripture of the New Testament. The earliest Christians did not have that spiritual advantage. Having those writings should make it much easier for us to have strong, vital, growing, powerful faiths. Look at all of our resources!

Is it not strange, then, that the Christian faith and the Christian church today are struggling? that in some places it barely survives? Many congregations are lifeless. They only go through the motions of "church." They have forgotten the passion and the joy of a life lived in the presence of Christ. Is Christ being denied? We want to say no, but let us reconsider.

Are we living lives that become the gospel? Are we living each day grasping the truth that God, through Jesus Christ, has brought us back into an eternally reconciled relationship? Are we living out lives of bold and strong love, sharing what we know to be true of Jesus Christ? As individuals and as families, are we living as though Christ's death and resurrection make any difference to us? Or have we reduced the Christian gospel to a nice list of moral behavior and think that if we are good, we will go to heaven?

The antichrist is one who denies the fact of faith that Jesus is the Son of God and all that it means. If there is any time in which we live in such a way that we show the world and ourselves that faith in Christ makes no difference at all, how much better off are we than an antichrist?

The gospel is indeed denied in many places in our world today. Many persons would say that life is hopeless. They would say that the only thing that counts is what you can hold in your hand. We as the followers of the risen Christ should do all in our power to answer such denial with the truth of Christ's love in our words and actions.

We must intentionally live lives that become the proclamation of God's good news to this world. We do not need to preach or knock on doors with witness tracts. It is simply a matter of looking honestly at our lives. Would anyone else in this world know we are Christian by our words, our actions, and our hope?

Our churches should also be on the forefront of proclaiming the gospel through our corporate word and acts. Would it make any difference to your community if your church suddenly disappeared? If not, then why not? Is your church a place of peace and an amplifier of hope in Christ to your town or city? When your church acts, is it to be a good group of citizens, or is it to witness to the saving power of the resurrected Christ? How can we expect our world and our neighbors to receive the love and grace of God unless we are there to share it with them?

It may not be so much a matter of a forceful denial of Christ as it is a matter of our apathy that then allows others who forcefully speak against God's love and grace to win.

WORDS FOR MY LIFE

Imagine if you were identified as an antichrist. Your whole life is defined by what you are not. Even if you are a great singer or a financial whiz, whether your home is in good shape or you vote in every election, you are, most importantly, someone who stands against the gospel: "anti-Christ."

How bleak it must be to be known only as someone who is against, or anti something. Turn the image around. Imagine you were identified as a Christian. How would anyone know? What does your faith do for you? How does it mold and shape your life?

What you and I believe of the gospel is the most fundamental belief we may ever hold—more important than political, environmental, cultural, economic, or even family understandings. What we come to know and trust in our lives to be our relationship with God through Jesus Christ carries us and stays with us through even our death.

Perhaps, as the writer of First John says, "the last hour" has come. Antichrists are in the world today. There have always been, and will continue to be, forces and persons who wish to destroy the unstoppable kingdom of God from coming into fullness on this earth.

Our simple task as the followers of Christ is to do also what the writer wrote: Let what we have heard abide in us. Allow the true, freeing, and gracious good news of God live within us. Let us confirm over and over again that it makes a difference that we are Christian. Hope, forgiveness, love, and eternal life become gifts to be cherished. The power of those who would diminish or destroy the gospel vanishes in the face of the abiding Christ.

23

What Will Heaven Be Like?

Revelation 21:1-7

Then I saw a new heaven and a new earth; for the first heaven and the first earth had passed away, and the sea was no more.

Revelation 21:1

WORDS FOR BIBLE TIMES

John received a vision. He recorded the revelation in order to strengthen the faith and the hope of Christians in Asia Minor. Those Christians were on the verge of tremendous persecution for their faith at the hands of the Romans. Many fascinating images appear in this revelation. Scholars and students have studied and tried to interpret those images for centuries.

One of the images is the picture in which God creates "a new heaven" and "a new earth," as the old creations are wiped away. These new creations will have none of the limitations of the old, for they are created to fit the fullness of God's kingdom that will never end. Christ is the centerpiece of that kingdom, ruling eternally with God. A new era begins for the universe.

What a great image! Unfortunately, we have, over the centuries, misread this Scripture text. If you were to ask people what heaven will look like, they would probably respond in terms of "pearly gates" and "streets of gold." If you look at the text in Revelation 21, however, very little detail is given to what the new heaven will look like. Instead, John talks about the New Jerusalem, which will come down from heaven as a creation of God. The New Jerusalem will be the place where God will dwell with God's people.

In the section of Scripture following the passage we are studying in this lesson (in Revelation 21:15-21), John describes the New Jerusalem. It is here that we find the gates of pearl and the golden streets. These are not building materials for heaven, but for the New Jerusalem!

Why does there need to be a "New Jerusalem"? The Book of Revelation was probably written after A.D. 70, when Roman legions destroyed the Temple. Most of the city of Jerusalem lay in ruins. Christians who understood the importance of Jerusalem within the Jewish roots of their faith knew that the destruction of Jerusalem was not the final word. God would rebuild and recreate the city as the eternal home.

We can read the Scripture, however, and find some important promises about our future with God. What does John tell us? "See, the home of God is among mortals." In John's revelation, at this point in history, God will once and for all remove any distance between us and God. God will always be with us, beside us. God will wipe away every tear. Death itself is eliminated. There will be no more mourning, nor crying, nor pain. That sounds pretty wonderful.

Whether it is in a New Jerusalem or in heaven, certainly God is providing a place of peace and wholeness for the children of God. It is a place of completion, where the longings of the human heart are filled, as in verse 6: "To the thirsty I will give water as a gift from the spring of the water of life." It is an eternal place, with a quality of existence that is far and away greater than the people of God have ever imagined. Eternity is more than simply a life that never ends. It is a way of existence lived in the very presence of God, as God chooses to dwell with humans for all time and beyond.

All this, as John saw it, comes after a universal and cosmic change. Part of the key to understanding the Book of Revelation is to know that John saw the terrible and devastating persecution that was moving toward the Christians. Indeed, to simply set up the Christians against Rome would mean certain elimination of the Christian faith. John's belief, however, was that God would intervene on behalf of the faithful. God would use the impending devastation as an opportunity to recreate the world. God would destroy those who wanted to destroy the faithful. If the believers will only hold fast to the faith that has been given to them, John asserts, then certainly God will come to the rescue and in the process bring a brand-new creation, in which all the horrible things that are about to happen will cease to exist. Peace, joy, and God's abiding presence will be all that remains. That's heaven, no matter where you are.

WORDS FOR OUR TIME

On license plates of cars from West Virginia, you will find the slogan "Almost Heaven." Taking the words from the song John Denver wrote while traveling in the Shenandoah River Valley and recorded back in the early 1970's, West Virginia has laid claim to the title of this particular piece of real estate. The only problem with that assertion, however, is that most of the folks from West Virginia obviously have never spent time in the Dakotas! If they would come to the upper Midwest (not necessarily in the dead of winter), they would probably have to go back and amend their license plates to read "Nearly Almost Heaven. See the Dakotas for More Information."

Many places around our country and around our world claim the title of "God's Country." When we visit those spots, we find ourselves breathless as we view the natural wonders and the sunsets. That which amazes us and takes our breath away is simply God's creation, the expression of God's creative love. When we think about heaven, then, we try to use the best and finest images we can imagine: it will be a place that is clean and fresh, perhaps with pearls, gold, and angel feathers. Heaven will be a banquet, or a park, or like the "City of Oz." Our human words attempt to describe the unbridled, unlimited, creative love of God.

Imagine what renovation work we would have to do in order to turn our own small corners of the world into heaven itself. Granted, again, some of us are blessed to live in places that are "almost" heaven. They are just "almost," however. As much as we might want to imagine heaven as that physically wonderful place, or eternity as that temporally wonderful time, they are neither. Heaven can be imagined in as many different ways as you like. The truth is, however, it can only be defined as existing wholly and unhesitatingly within the love of God. Artificial heavens can only be artificial.

As we live in faith on earth, we work hard to create a sense of that loving presence of God. Our prayers are that we might grow closer to God. We want to be in the arms of Christ. We want to hear Christ's voice. We desire to witness and feel God's love always present with us, no matter what else comes.

Indeed, there are moments and even periods of life when we feel "almost" there. Those times ebb and flow, however, as our spiritual life and growth go through cycles of closeness and separation. We will only experience eternity in its completeness and heaven in its total beauty when God brings them to pass. The questions of what heaven will be like and what eternity will be like remain for us as points of hope as we look to the future. God is in charge of the future, and it will be one bright with hope. We, like the early Christians, should be able to gain the strength that comes from hope to meet the struggles of today, knowing that "sometime" and "somewhere" we will receive the gifts beyond time and place.

WORDS FOR MY LIFE

The week that I wrote this lesson, I turned forty years old. I had always taken great pleasure in reminding persons of their significant birthdays and of the change that was occurring in their lives. I do not think I will do that again for a while. Although some of you reading this will scoff at the fact that I am "only forty," my birthday brought a twinge and a sense of loss, even a bit of mourning and pain. It was nothing specific, just simply a part of growing older; but it was still there. It would be enough, if I could only be granted one day in my entire life when there would be no mourning, no pain, no crying. It would be enough if I could live that day in the certain knowledge that it was that day and so would be freed from the fear or the expectation that those things might occur.

This is the human condition. Sometimes the hardness of life comes as we are persecuted and hammered on by those forces that would enjoy taking our life and faith away. Sometimes we live lives that are less than abundant, far less than eternal in their quality, because it hurts to be human. Life brings pain, tears, loss, and fear. Those things rob us of the peace and joy that should be ours as followers of Christ, we think.

When we stop for a moment and look at the gifts that have been laid before us in our lives, however, we may come to understand just how well God has cared for us in our human lives. Granted, life brings pain, but life also brings times of great joy and love and brave sharing of truth. Christ has promised for us to have an abundant life, abundant in the assurance that God is for us even in the struggles we go through. Even more important, what we have to go through now in our lives is hardly worth comparing with the eternal life that is promised to us. Heaven, or the new Earth, or the New Jerusalem is laid out as a promise. Even greater is the promise that for all eternity, God will abide with the people of God—God's home will be with us. That is the best news we will ever hear.